PRISONER OF THE SWISS

PRISONER OF THE SWISS

A World War II Airman's Story

DAN CULLER
with ROB MORRIS
Foreword by DWIGHT S. MEARS

CASEMATE
Philadelphia & Oxford

Published in the United States of America and Great Britain in 2017 by
CASEMATE PUBLISHERS
1950 Lawrence Road, Havertown, PA 19083, USA
and
The Old Music Hall, 106–108 Cowley Road, Oxford OX4 1JE, UK

Copyright 2017 © Daniel Culler, Rob Morris and Dwight Mears

Hardcover Edition: ISBN 978-1-61200-554-6
Digital Edition: ISBN 978-1-61200-555-3

A CIP record for this book is available from the British Library and the Library of Congress

All rights reserved. No part of this book may be reproduced or transmitted in any form or by
any means, electronic or mechanical including photocopying, recording or by any information
storage and retrieval system, without permission from the publisher in writing.

Printed and bound in the United States of America

For a complete list of Casemate titles, please contact:

CASEMATE PUBLISHERS (US)
Telephone (610) 853-9131
Fax (610) 853-9146
Email: casemate@casematepublishers.com
www.casematepublishers.com

CASEMATE PUBLISHERS (UK)
Telephone (01865) 241249
Email: casemate-uk@casematepublishers.co.uk
www.casematepublishers.co.uk

Contents

Foreword: The Historical and Legal Origins of Swiss Neutrality
   Dwight S. Mears   vii
Final Notes on Swiss Neutrality
   Rob Morris   xii
Editor's Note to the 2017 Revised Edition   xvi

Part I: The Black Hole of Wauwilermoos

1	Beginnings	3
2	Combat	19
3	Missions	24
4	Shot Down and Internment Camp	33
5	Interned at Adelboden	40
6	The First Escape	44
7	Entering the Gates of Hell	49
8	The Depths of Despair	55
9	Hospital	66
10	The Second Escape	70
11	Out of the Depths	79
12	The Return to England	82
13	Interrogation in London	86
14	Home Again	91
15	Endings	94

vi • CONTENTS

16	The Black Hole of Wauwilermoos Returns	98
17	Appendix to the Original 1995 Edition of *The Black Hole of Wauwilermoos*	101

Part II: Aftermath
Rob Morris and Dwight S. Mears

18	Moving On	109
19	André Béguin and General Barnwell Rhett Legge	110
20	Recognition at Last	113

Selected Bibliography and Sources   121

FOREWORD

The Historical and Legal Origins of Swiss Neutrality

Dr. Dwight S. Mears, Former Assistant Professor of History, United States Military Academy at West Point

Dr. Mears received a B.A. degree from the U.S. Military Academy at West Point in 2001, an M.A. from the University of North Carolina at Chapel Hill in 2010, and a PhD from the University of North Carolina at Chapel Hill in 2012. He also cross-enrolled in the UNC Law School to gain more exposure to international law. His dissertation focused on the internment of American airmen in Switzerland during World War II and the consequences for the International Law of Armed Conflict. He is an Army major with a background in aviation and military intelligence. Mears, who is also a pilot, currently teaches American history at West Point. The views expressed in this book are those of the author and do not reflect the official policy or position of the Department of the Army, Department of Defense, or the U.S. government.

This is the story of a U.S. airman who endured a number of difficult experiences during World War II: the trauma of combat, captivity in a neutral nation, and the lingering psychological and physiological effects that burdened him after the war's conclusion. Dan Culler's story is gripping because he suffered more than most Americans who were interned in Switzerland, and his account lays bare the personal toll of his experience.

It will be instructive to preface Dan's story with some context on the origins of internment as well as its application in Switzerland. Before they were permanent neutrals, the Swiss Confederation was offensive.

viii • FOREWORD

This gradually changed by the 17th century when military losses convinced the Confederation to stay out of the wars of their more populous European neighbors. However, they also realized that abstaining from armed conflicts—or declaring neutrality—gave them the opportunity to provide services as an "active neutral" for the belligerent parties, such as humanitarian assistance and acting as an intermediary for powers who had no diplomatic relations. The internment of belligerents grew out of these practices, as the Swiss realized that providing asylum for soldiers was most equitable if they were interned for the duration of the conflict; preventing a return to the battlefield was necessary to avoid complaints by other warring parties. The Swiss first instituted internment in the War of 1859, utilized it again in 1871 during the Franco-Prussian War, and later codified it in treaty law in the 1899 Hague Convention (II) with Respect to the Laws and Customs of War on Land as well as the 1907 Hague Convention (V) respecting the Rights and Duties of Neutral Powers and Persons in Case of War on Land. Therefore, during the global conflicts of the 20th century, Switzerland interned soldiers as required by international law.

During World War II, Dan Culler was only one of over 100,000 military refugees of belligerent countries who received asylum in Switzerland. Of this number, only 1,517 internees were U.S. service members, all of whom arrived via aircraft. This was the largest group of U.S. airmen interned in any neutral country in the war; the next closest tally was in Sweden, which interned 1,218 U.S. flyers. The massive numbers of aircrew who sought refuge in Switzerland and Sweden prompted speculation that at least some of these men had landed intentionally without sufficient cause, such as crippling combat damage or significant malfunction that would prevent a return to base. In the summer of 1944 the neutral landings were investigated at the direction of the commanding general of the USAAF, Gen. Henry H. Arnold, and no aircrew were found to have interned themselves dishonorably. However, the misperception that many internees were cowards survived in popular memory due to wartime rumors fed by enemy propaganda as well as popular literature.

Most neutral countries in Europe found various pretexts to release U.S. airmen from internment, particularly by 1944 when the fortunes of war favored the Allies. However, Switzerland took its internment obligations under The Hague Conventions more seriously than other neutrals. This was due to a combination of factors: Swiss neutrality had significant cultural value to its population; the Swiss themselves were tasked with upholding the laws of armed conflict in other countries; and many in the Swiss government were nervous about possible German reprisals for overlooking internment obligations. Therefore, when interned soldiers attempted to flee the country, the Swiss government believed that such attempts jeopardized their neutrality and were not amused. In the fall of 1944, hundreds of U.S. airmen attempted escape after the Allied forces that invaded occupied France reached the western border of Switzerland.

The U.S. airmen had varied motives for escape. Many were dutifully following War Department policy, which had been briefed to them at their bases before they were interned. Others simply wanted to rejoin families, spouses, or girlfriends. They often attempted escape on their own without the assistance of U.S. authorities, largely because the Legation had little communication, much less direct command and control, with the airmen. While the Legation staff were in Bern, the airmen were interned in various remote mountain camps. This lack of communication led to an acrimonious relationship between many internees and the Legation staff, as the internees almost universally perceived that U.S. officials failed to adequately assist them. In reality the Legation was secretly coordinating escapes, but had an insufficient staff that also handled many other important diplomatic and intelligence-related functions.

The Swiss Army interdicted many of the would-be escapees, particularly those who escaped without U.S. government assistance. The airmen were often incarcerated in local jails, and later transferred to prison camps. The worst of these camps was Wauwilermoos, where at least 161 U.S. airmen were sent for the honorable offense of attempted escape. However, not all of the camp's occupants were honorable offenders, as the facility also housed criminals from the entire population of military refugees. Some internees, like Dan Culler, suffered egregious mistreatment at the camp, while many others endured an unpleasant period of confinement and emerged malnourished and diseased. Most

Swiss citizens and government officials were completely unaware of the extreme conditions at Wauwilermoos, and even responsible military officials were largely ignorant of the camp's mismanagement by a corrupt Nazi sympathizer.

Therefore, the Swiss government's culpability in the camp's conditions is subjectively a product of omission, since they failed to appoint competent leadership and supervise the administration of the camp. Adding to the confusion was the fact that the Geneva Convention of 1929 relative to the Treatment of Prisoners of War did not formally cover internees in neutral countries. Therefore, somewhat paradoxically, Swiss military officials refused to afford military internees the same standards of treatment and legal protections that they were upholding in prisoner of war camps of warring nations.

The mistreatment of U.S. airmen in Wauwilermoos eventually sparked a diplomatic confrontation between the Swiss authorities and the U.S. Legation in Bern. A formal protest was authorized by the U.S. State Department, who accused the Swiss of violating the laws of armed conflict. A compromise resulted wherein the Swiss Federal Council released most incarcerated U.S. airmen on parole, and later confined them in less punitive facilities. This was a product of strong advocacy by the U.S. Legation, although the role of U.S. officials was largely unknown to most of the internees.

Hundreds of U.S. airmen successfully escaped from Switzerland, and those who did not were repatriated in a POW exchange near the war's conclusion. Many who spent time in Wauwilermoos left with ambivalent feelings about the experience; whilst they were well treated by the overwhelmingly pro-Allied population of Switzerland, they also experienced what they saw as unnecessarily draconian treatment for attempting escape. The majority blamed the Swiss authorities for allowing such a camp to exist, as well as the U.S. government for failing to provide escape assistance or secure their release earlier.

After the war, most internees perceived a lasting stigma, a vestige of the wartime misperception that they had intentionally evaded combat and enjoyed a tranquil ski-vacation in the mountains. This stigma was exacerbated by popular literature.

Wartime novels such as Ernest Hemingway's *A Farewell to Arms* and Joseph Heller's *Catch-22* recycled the theme of soldiers plotting to escape to Switzerland and leave combat behind. Some amateur and scholarly historians also fanned the flames by repeating the wartime rumors as fact. The stigma likely influenced protracted delays in the internees' receipt of VA benefits and the military decoration of the POW Medal. Dan Culler and the other U.S. internees who were held in Wauwilermoos for attempted escape are now eligible for these medical benefits and the POW Medal as a result of how they were treated in captivity, but both the benefits and decorations were only attained after statutory amendments to federal law explicitly clarified that captives of neutrals were eligible for consideration. Unfortunately, the amendments came on April 30, 2014—too late for many, but it is never too late to remedy this sort of wrong.

It is my hope that the republication of this book will promote wider recognition of what Dan and other U.S. internees experienced. In turn, this will help erase the stigma of internment, and perhaps help these men come to terms with the unpleasant memories of their time in Switzerland.

Final Notes on Swiss Neutrality

Rob Morris

With the creation of the collaborationist Vichy French government in 1942, all rail service between Switzerland and the free world was cut. It was completely surrounded by nations that were either fascist or under fascist control.

Switzerland, roughly the size of Maryland, is a tiny landlocked nation in the center of Europe. Because of its central location, it is a cultural mosaic with four official languages. Roughly 65 percent of Swiss speak German, 22.5 percent speak French, 8.4 percent speak Italian, and 0.6 percent speak a language called Romansh. Traditionally, the Swiss economy has been strong, based on high-end precision manufactured goods and banking.

In 1939, Switzerland mobilized an army and air force of 850,000 men, warning that an attack on Swiss neutrality would result in war. If Germany was going to invade, it would pay dearly in blood and materiel.

In 1940, the Swiss Air Force consisted of 262 French Morane-Saulnier fighters and 99 German-built Messerschmitt Bf-109 fighters. These were first used against Germany in 1940 when German aircraft violated Swiss airspace during attacks on France. Swiss fighters scrambled and shot down German aircraft. In June 1940, German Luftwaffe Chief Hermann Göring launched a retaliatory commando raid to blow up Swiss air bases at Payerne and Dübendorf. After the Swiss captured the commandos, Göring threatened to cut off German coal deliveries unless Switzerland returned its entire fleet of Messerschmitts. The Swiss refused. He then pushed for air strikes, but Germany had other things on its plate and the attacks were never approved by German high command.

FINAL NOTES ON SWISS NEUTRALITY • xiii

The British Royal Air Force also violated Swiss airspace on bombing missions to Italy. Switzerland protested, but usually shot to miss—until December 16, 1940, when RAF bombers targeting Mannheim, Germany, accidentally bombed the Swiss city of Basel, nearly 140 miles away. Just three nights later, the Swiss contested an RAF flyover, firing on a bomber formation on its way to Milan.

In August 1943, an RAF Mark IV Mosquito, one of the most advanced high-altitude fighters in the world, equipped with the latest RAF navigational equipment, made a forced landing after experiencing engine trouble. Intense negotiations followed. The Swiss refused to return it, instead making it a Swiss Air Mail carrier.

In the summer of 1943, the British and Americans began the new strategy of "round-the-clock bombing"—the British would area bomb by night, and the Americans would precision bomb in daylight. Since many German targets were close to Switzerland, airspace violations increased dramatically. Allied bombers also began intentionally diverting to Switzerland after being hit or experiencing severe mechanical trouble. Swiss policy in such circumstances was to send four fighters to intercept and guide the offender to a landing field, usually Dübendorf.

On April 28, 1944, a German Bf-110G night fighter and crew experiencing engine trouble landed at Dübendorf, equipped with the newest radar and night-fighter weapons system, the latest codes, and with the creator of German night-fighter strategy on the crew. The Luftwaffe went into panic mode, even considering a commando raid. In the end, the plane was destroyed in front of German witnesses in exchange for 12 Messerschmitt Bf-109Gs, for which the Swiss paid 500,000 gold francs, repatriation for the three crewmen, and 20,000 highly desirable Swiss cigarettes.

On April 1, 1944, 38 American B-24 bombers accidentally bombed the Swiss city of Shauffhausen, near Lake Constance, killing 40 Swiss civilians. From then on, Switzerland ordered that no U.S. or RAF aircraft would be allowed to fly closer than 50 miles from the Swiss border in good weather and 150 miles in bad weather.

On February 22, 1945, Shauffhausen was bombed again, and 10 days after that, nine B-24s targeting Freiburg bombed Basel, while six more bombed Zurich. Eighth Air Force commander General Carl Spaatz was ordered to go to Switzerland armed with an explanation and an apology.

By the war's end in May, Switzerland had documented 6,501 violations of Swiss airspace, 4,000 of them in the war's final months. Switzerland had been bombed 89 times, killing or wounding nearly 350 Swiss. Swiss fighters shot down 26 Allied or Axis aircraft. In all, 218 Allied or Axis aircraft crashed or landed in Switzerland.

A total of 166 American aircraft were interned in Switzerland. Eighty-two were B-24s, 74 were B-17s, and the remainder were a smattering of other types. Forty-one aircraft were categorized as destroyed in crashes, 39 landed badly damaged, and 86 landed in repairable condition. The first American plane to land was the 93rd Bomb Group's B-24 "Death Dealer," on March 16, 1944. The last was a 30th Bomb Group B-17 named "Princess O'Rourke," on April 20, 1945. The record day for new arrivals was March 18, 1944, when 16 American planes landed.

In total 1,516 Americans were interned in Switzerland during the war. Additional Americans arrived in Switzerland after evading and had evadee status, which gave them greater freedom of movement. The internees, most of whom landed at the Swiss air base of Dübendorf, were assigned to one of three internment camps created for the purpose— Adelboden, Wengen, and Davos. These were hard-to-reach villages in the Swiss Alps, and escape from any of them was difficult. Internees were housed in Swiss resort hotels, minus many of the pre-war amenities. The American government paid the Swiss for the internees' upkeep and each man even got a small stipend. Life was not harsh, despite a lack of freedom and food. Men were allowed to ski, ride bikes, hike, and interact with the local population. They were not, however, allowed to try to escape.

Sixty Americans lost their lives in Switzerland. Twenty-seven were killed by Swiss antiaircraft guns or fighters; others were killed in crashes. Two men committed suicide while interned.

German aircraft also landed and were interned in Switzerland. Because of the ease of escape back to Germany, many German airmen escaped. However, 783 elected to remain in Switzerland for the war's duration.

Most internees had fairly pleasant stays in Switzerland. The exceptions were those who tried to escape. By the end of the war, as the Allied lines became easier to reach, roughly 70 percent of the Americans did escape. Early on, when Dan Culler made his first attempt, Switzerland was surrounded by hostile nations, and success was unlikely. The punishment for escape or attempted escape was jail time. Some ended up in the Swiss federal prison at Wauwilermoos, which was administered by a sadistic Swiss Nazi and embezzler named André Béguin.

Editor's Note to the 2017 Revised Edition

Dan Culler's *The Black Hole of Wauwilermoos* first came out in 1995. It was self-published, written in a burst of creative energy over a three-month period during which Dan sometimes worked day and night. A small print run of 1,000 books resulted, and were quickly sold out. Despite its small scale and lack of promotion, *The Black Hole of Wauwilermoos* has become a book that is widely admired and often quoted by World War II scholars and historians, most recently in Donald Miller's best-selling *Masters of the Air*.

I met Dan back in 2000, when I was researching a book on the European air war. I'd never heard of Swiss internment or of the ordeals suffered by some of the interned airmen. With the help of Swiss Internees Association President Bob Long, I interviewed half a dozen for the book. One man's story was so powerful that it got its own chapter. That was Dan's. I also gained a good friend.

I have attempted to stay true to the book's original premise and style. All I've done is tighten it up (it's about half as long as the original). If, upon finishing, one is left wanting more, I recommend the original version of *Black Hole*, and Dan's memoir of his childhood and young adulthood, *The Circle of Thorns: Birth and Learning Years*.

Dan was a prolific and thoughtful writer of short stories, poems, and books, most of which he shared only with a few friends. Reading Dan's collected works has allowed me to get to know a man who was at the core intensely guarded and private, a man deeply impacted by his wartime experiences, who carried with him a multitude of physical and emotional scars that will never heal. Despite his having lived through the banality and evil of war and imprisonment, despite being betrayed by his own government, he continued to courageously reach out to others. Given every reason to reject a loving God and a rational universe, he remained a spiritual man.

Dan Culler passed away April 24, 2016, in Green Valley, Arizona, at the age of 92.

Rob Morris
Ammon, Idaho, June 2017

Part I
The Black Hole of Wauwilermoos

Dan Culler

I wish to dedicate this book to my wife Betty, who has always stood beside me when I needed someone. I am also grateful for the support of my daughters, Sandra, Diana, and Deborah. I also want to thank my deceased mother who, with her strong Quaker beliefs, was against war but never questioned my going and who, after I returned, tried to heal the pain with loving care and understanding.

Dan Culler
Tucson, Arizona, 1990

CHAPTER I

Beginnings

I was born March 22, 1924, in Syracuse, Indiana, the tenth child of Maude and Clement Culler. We actually had 12 children, but two died in their first years of life by what was commonly called in those days "the one-year death sickness." My mother was the daughter of Irish immigrants, and like most mothers in those days, she was the silent rock who held our family together. My father was descended from German Pennsylvania Dutch Dunkards [a sect similar to the Mennonites]. He was a brilliant man, gifted in many things, much to his detriment, for it led to a lifetime of dissatisfaction—a longing to see what was over the next hill or around the next corner. He was deeply spiritual, endlessly searching to fill what he perceived as a void deep within his soul. Before I was born, he abandoned the family to go to California and follow the prophet Billy Sunday. He just up and left, trusting in the Lord to watch over his wife and six young children; he believed that if he was doing God's work, God would care for them in return.

Thankfully, he also left behind a 4-acre truck farm, and through sheer force of will, hard work, and with the help of the children, Mother was able to keep the family afloat, all the while praying that Father would come to his senses and discover what she already knew—Billy Sunday was a fraud.

About the time she'd decided Father was never coming back, she got a letter from California begging forgiveness and enough money for a train ticket home. She gave in on one condition: the next time he took off to follow some religious nut, he needn't bother asking for either forgiveness or a ticket home.

Father moved on from Billy Sunday, but remained deeply religious. He was known in the area for walking behind his plow in the fields, one hand on the plow, the other gripping an open Bible. Most considered him a religious fanatic. To his credit, he worked hard, 12 hours a day, six days a week, splitting his time between the farm and his job as a millwright in a Syracuse factory.

Farm children in those days worked like slaves, and we were no exception. We worked and had little time for recreation. Mother also worked hard, supervising the truck farm through its seasonal cycles of planting, cultivating, picking, and then selling the produce or canning 1,000 two-quart jars of fruits and vegetables a year.

We referred to the farm, idealistically, as "our house on the hill." The house sat back from the road, atop a rise, above Milford Road. In my boyhood, it became a magical place where I could gaze for miles across the verdant green pastures and dream about the places I'd go someday.

Father, like many honest but poor Americans, dreamed big dreams that were never fulfilled. He worked dawn to dusk and tried to make all the right decisions, but it seemed that every time he was on the cusp of success, such as getting a better piece of machinery or building an addition, another baby was born, or someone would get sick with an illness requiring a big doctor's bill. His harshness, his anger, was a direct result of his disappointment. Instead of blaming himself for his failure, he blamed his family for holding him back.

One March morning in 1926, when I was nearly two years old, Mother was about to lift the hinged double-doors into the basement when she heard something thump into our house's front window. She rushed to look and found a dove lying on the ground. Thinking it was dead, she reached down to touch it, and it burst back to life with beating wings and flew north, toward the road and the railroad tracks. Amazed by its quick recovery, she watched the dove as it circled over the tracks, turned and then flew back toward our house, dashing itself a second time against the front window. It fell to earth, roused itself, and flew to the railroad tracks a second time, where it circled before winging away to the north.

Mother watched till the dove was a distant speck in the steel gray sky, then started her descent into the basement, her skin crawling. She told Father when he got home from work. Father was taking the following day off from work to do farm business, and she begged him to be careful as he drove the dirt country roads, especially where the roads crossed the railroad tracks. Father assured her that he would, and told her she was letting her imagination get the best of her.

The next afternoon, my sister and brother, 10 and eight, were riding home from school in the school bus when they came to the railroad crossing near our house. The bus driver stopped, as was the law, and one of the kids got off and looked up and down the tracks for a train, climbing back in and saying one was coming. While they waited, my brother and sister saw our father's touring car approaching from the west on the Milford Road, and they proudly told the other kids. They watched him approach, noticing he was not slowing down or looking down the tracks. He drove his car onto the tracks just as the fast-moving B&O Capital Limited passenger train passed by. There was a deafening, metal-tearing impact as the two collided, followed by sparks and screeching as the engine dragged what was left of the car half a mile down the tracks before stopping. Bystanders pulled Father's battered body from the mangled wreckage, surprised to find he still had a spark of life; he died hours later at the hospital in Elkhart, leaving his family alone to deal with the future.

Before Father's shattered corpse was even buried in the ground, the railroad presented Mother with a bill for damage to the train engine's cow catcher and for lost revenue from the delay caused by the accident in the amount of $500. This was an amount of money that would be ruinous to pay, and the railroad bullied Mother for a long time after, even threatening to take away her farm, but they never collected. The railroad was heartless. In a separate incident, it sent an unemployed man to jail for six months for "stealing coal" that had fallen from the coal car onto the sides of the tracks so that he could feed his family. He was arrested with five pieces of coal in his gunnysack.

I did many different jobs growing up. One of my earliest was helping Mother clean the cottages of the rich at Lake Wawasee before they showed up for the summer season. I was fascinated that kids had so many beautiful toys that they only played with a few months a year. Though Mother never let me play with the toys, I was allowed to push the wheeled ones across the floor on their journey to the toy boxes.

Mother remarried, hoping for a provider to pitch in and help with our large family. Sadly, my stepfather was a lazy good-for-nothing who chewed tobacco, cussed up a storm, and spent his days sitting by the stove spitting streams of tobacco juice into a metal pail. In 1929, the country plunged into the darkest days of the Great Depression. Poor people and hoboes criss-crossed the land, and there was a general feeling of fear, gnawing hunger, and imminent disaster and decay. The Roosevelt Administration offered a job to any man willing to work with a new program called the Works Progress Administration, or WPA. The WPA's job in Syracuse was to hand-dig trenches for a new town sewer system. When it was completed, raw sewage would no longer be dumped directly into Turkey Creek or the nearby lakes. My stepfather refused to work for the WPA, insisting that it wasn't "real work" but government make-work, and that WPA workers were all lazy and did nothing but lean on their shovels all day. Instead, he stayed home and sat by the kitchen stove, chewing and spitting tobacco and ordering us around.

I had a paper route and also sold our produce door-to-door, and one day, while visiting at my Aunt Lillian and Uncle Vern's house, I was greeted by the cutest little white puppies I'd ever seen. I just knew I had to have one of those puppies. Aunt Lillian said she'd saved one just for me, and showed me a pup with black patches around his eyes. We took to one another instantly. At first, my stepfather wouldn't agree, saying the dog would be just another mouth to feed, but Mother won out and I got to keep the little dog, whom we named Toby. Toby was allowed to eat leftovers from the table, and for the first week, he had to sleep in the barn. Mother let me sleep out there with him. Both of us were scared, but we snuggled close together, and it wasn't long before Toby was allowed to sleep on the day bed under the side porch. On cold nights, I would take a blanket and go sleep with him.

I. BEGINNINGS • 7

Toby rode with me on my produce deliveries, in a makeshift basket attached to the wagon, and it seemed that with him along, the route went fast and his happy grin encouraged people to buy more.

By high school, I had a good job working at Macy's, a marina at Lake Wawasee, working on Chris-Craft boats and motors. These would be bought or rented out by the wealthy folks who came to the lake in the summertime. War had broken out in Europe, but it seemed a long way off and of little importance to Americans. Nobody was concerned about Japanese aggression in the Pacific. Most Americans, being of European descent, were more concerned with the war in Europe. German-Americans, early on, seemed to support Germany. The Germans had excellent propaganda; they'd held a giant Nazi rally at Madison Square Garden in the late thirties. The Culler ancestors were German, but they were Dunkards, and were totally against war of any kind. Even though Mother's ancestors were Irish, she agreed with the Quaker belief that no man has the right to take another's life for any reason.

Every moment I wasn't working Toby and I would get in my old Model A and drive around the countryside. Sometimes we'd pull over late at night and turn off the headlights. If there was a full moon, you could see forever, rolling farmland bathed in pale blue light and lit up like day. On moonless nights, the stars would sparkle like diamonds on a sheet of velvet, and I'd look up and wonder what the future held, for the country and for me personally.

In November 1941, I traded the Model A for a beautiful dark green 1938 Ford four-door sedan for $150. Because I was underage, Mother signed for it. For the next several weeks, all I did was wash and polish that car. I was even reluctant to let Toby sit in it, because he was a shedder, and he dropped long white hair all over the soft cloth seats.

On December 7, 1941, three friends and I were watching a movie at the Lincoln Theater in Goshen. Halfway through the show, the projector was turned off and the house lights came on. A man walked onto the stage and announced that Japan had just bombed Pearl Harbor, Hawaii. None of us knew, at that time, where Pearl Harbor was. Thousands of Americans had been killed. As we left the theater, an old World War I veteran wearing his American Legion cap stood on the sidewalk telling anyone who would listen, "Tomorrow the Japs and Germans could be marching down Main Street!"

I wanted to sign up immediately, but Mother refused, first on religious grounds, and also because she was unconvinced that Roosevelt hadn't orchestrated the attack somehow to draw the United States into the war. She reminded anyone who would listen that he'd promised every American mother, in the last election, that no American son or daughter would be sent to fight on foreign soil. For the rest of her life, she never forgave him for breaking this promise.

I soon discovered that if I went to South Bend, I could sign up at 17, but my mother would have to sign the papers when I was called up. Mother couldn't believe that after all her preaching, and all my church learning, that I could even consider going and killing my fellow men in Roosevelt's war, but I was determined. It was my duty. The world was threatened and the cause was just. Being a conscientious objector or getting a deferment as an essential farm worker never even crossed my mind.

In January 1942 I went to South Bend and signed up with the Army Air Corps. The recruiter doubted I'd be called up before I was 18. He said it would take the country a while to build training bases and housing for all the enlistees and draftees.

Four months later I got a telegram instructing me to report to the armory at South Bend for my physical and induction. Before Mother and I left, I took a day off so that I could get my car ready for my prolonged absence, putting it up on jacks, running the oil out of the pistons, and putting logs under each axle so that the car's tires wouldn't touch the ground.

Toby and I went for one last walk together. He stuck to me like glue, and we walked for miles through our favorite woods, fields, and creeks. I talked to him like I'd talk to my closest friend, which he was. He walked just ahead of me, turning and cocking his head to listen while I caught up. That night, we slept on the porch, looking up at the stars, listening to the whistle of the train for the last time. The next morning, as I pulled away in the car, I looked back and saw Toby standing on the high bank across the lane from the house. He watched me as we disappeared from sight.

The armory in South Bend was a madhouse. I filled out lots of papers, took a physical, and claimed Mother as my dependent. This way, she would receive 50 dollars a month out of my private's paycheck. My mother reluctantly signed my enlistment papers, grimly commenting that she felt like she was signing my death warrant.

In a scene repeated hundreds of thousands of times all over the country, and millions of times all over the world, I watched as husbands and wives, boyfriends and girlfriends, fathers and children, sons and parents, tearfully said their goodbyes, reluctant to let go, not knowing if they would ever touch again. My thoughts went back to my church teaching—that war and hate will bring only death, sadness, separation, and loneliness, while love and trust will bring life, togetherness, happiness, and peace. As I boarded the bus, I wondered to myself why man fights wars.

When I signed up for the service in January 1942, I knew very little about American military life. I knew several men who had joined up during the Depression, but that was in order to keep their families from starving. I'd never been more than 30 miles from our farmhouse in my life. Basic training was at Atlantic City, New Jersey. We spent our days drilling and learning the Army way of doing things. Most of us younger recruits learned the general orders without much difficulty, but the older recruits would argue and complain that they couldn't see the point of this garbage. From Atlantic City, I went by train to Lincoln, Nebraska. We had to pull the blinds at every station so that civilians on the platform couldn't see it was a troop train. We rarely knew where we were. Occasionally, someone would crack the blinds and recognize a landmark. I loved riding the train—the hypnotic clickety-clack, clickety-clack of the wheels passing over each joint, the slow rolling motion that lulled you to sleep like a baby being rocked in a cradle. I was assigned a lower bunk, and at night I cracked the blinds and lay on my stomach, gazing out at the countryside, at the lights of the farms, towns, and cities as we passed. Everything was new, exciting, and filled with great expectations. The notion that someone in another part of the world was training at that very moment to harm or kill me never crossed my mind. My thoughts were of adventure, seeing new things, doing new things, and making a difference in a struggle for the future of humanity. I suppose this is how most young men see things as they head off to war, though few of them return from war still feeling that way, and some never return at all.

As far as any of us knew, there *was* no military installation in Lincoln; however, it turned out that the Army had built a giant training base on the town's outskirts in a very short span of time, and it was one of the largest of hundreds that had sprung up all over the United States as we ramped up our war effort. At Lincoln, the Army had the unenviable job of bringing together thousands upon thousands of men from all over the United States, from every lifestyle and civilian occupation, and molding them into a unified fighting force.

It was winter, and the blizzards howled in full force across the Nebraska plains. The icy wind sliced through our coats as if they were made of paper. The worst time of day was 4 a.m. reveille, when in the frigid darkness the base bugler rousted us with his bleating call over the base intercom. Men hesitantly pushed off their warm blankets and touched their feet to the freezing concrete floor to make their way to the latrine before making their bunks. As we marched to the mess hall, our barracks sang a marching song—"How I hate to get up in the morning." To this day, whenever I walk outside on a cold winter morning, that song rises out of the vault of the distant past and into my consciousness.

Given the chance at Lincoln to sign up for specialized schooling, I chose to be on a combat flight crew. To qualify, I had to pass a special flying physical and take a series of tests. Three men in our barrack signed up, but I was the only one who passed all the tests.

The time in Lincoln passed quickly and soon graduation day was upon us. Everyone—even the older men with very little education—finished with good grades. The instructors were excellent, mostly older civilian men. I remember one in particular. He was Jewish, and he'd managed to escape from Nazi Germany. Many of us were interested in learning what was really going on in Germany. We'd heard things about how the Germans were treating the Jews. Were the Jews really being persecuted to the extent that the newspapers were reporting? At first, our teacher didn't want to talk about it, but after we pressed him, he told us that no matter what we read in the papers, what was happening in Europe was *a hundred times worse.* It was up to us, he said, to do everything possible to defeat the Germans, whom he referred to as "Nazi animals."

After graduation, I was assigned to the Consolidated Aircraft Plant in San Diego, California, a non-military factory school staffed by civilians whose job was to train personnel in the varied workings of the four-engine Consolidated B-24 Liberator heavy bomber. The B-24 was one of the Army's two large heavy bombers, the other being the Boeing B-17 Flying Fortress. The six-week school was accelerated due to heavy demand for air and ground crew members to fly America's newest heavy bomber. It was also a lot tougher. You had to learn fast, or you washed out. Every Friday was test day, and if you were still in camp on Monday, you knew that you'd passed the previous week's test. Each week there were fewer and fewer men at the school. I wished I'd paid better attention to some of my schooling back home, but I did manage to pass, and felt both proud and honored. When the six weeks were up, I was given orders to travel to Wendover, Nevada, for aerial gunnery school.

Wendover Gunnery School was located in one of the most remote places I'd ever seen, out in the middle of the desert directly west of Salt Lake City on the border with Nevada. The barracks were crudely built, each having its own outside latrine. Schooling started at once, and was accelerated and intense. Though the training was difficult, there was such a high demand for air crews that if the school noticed you had an eagerness to learn and a certain level of aptitude, they would stick with you. We were taught how to track an enemy fighter using the special sights on the machine guns, figuring, in a matter of seconds, the distance to the target from our plane and how much to lead it before firing. Bombers at this time were equipped with moveable turrets and supported by two .50-caliber guns. I learned how to operate the turret and how to repair it. Another part of our training was to be able to identify, in a split-second, the silhouettes of every plane, including German, Japanese, and Italian fighters and bombers and our own planes. This was a life and death lesson, though we learned after a few combat missions to shoot at anyone who pointed his nose at you.

12 • PRISONER OF THE SWISS

We spent mornings in the classroom, afternoons at target practice. First we shot at stationary targets, where we got used to the noise and the way the tracer shells flew into the target. We then graduated to moving targets. Ideally, we'd learn this skill from an open-cockpit plane, but it was early in the war and the Army needed every available aircraft to train pilots, not aerial gunners. Instead, we relied on an old railroad hand cart, the kind that is propelled by two men pushing up and down on a lever. The cart ran on a 500-foot track over undulating terrain, to give the sensation of turbulence, and had a .30-caliber gun mounted on a pedestal. Two students would pump the handle up and down to propel the cart, and a third would fire at stationary targets somewhat resembling airplanes and made of canvas that had been placed on a hill about a thousand feet from the track. Each student was assigned his own color of shells and the instructors could tally your score by counting the colored holes. Not hitting the target at all was grounds for flunking out of aerial gunnery, but by this point, we had come so far that it wasn't enforced. In fact, unless you hit the instructor instead of the side of the mountain, you were going to pass.

We were also supposed to do some skeet shooting, but never did. We had plenty of shotguns, but no shells and no clay pigeons, so another phase of gunnery training was skipped altogether. I heard one instructor lament to the sergeant in charge of the firing range: "If I were a German pilot, I'd want to fly against this first group of trainees. If there is someone watching over our flying men," he continued, "I pray He'll bless them with gut reaction when they meet the enemy, as their only training will be combat."

During the course, the Army became so desperate for more bomber crews that the six-week course was cut to three. At the end of three weeks, none of us had been taken up in an airplane! How were we supposed to know if we were able to stand heights, or who got airsick or had ear problems, if we never went aloft? We'd all heard reports of men who'd gone into combat, only to lose their stripes when it was discovered that they were prone to airsickness or couldn't handle the physical demands of high-altitude flight. Regardless, at the end of three weeks, we were awarded our shiny silver aerial gunner's wings and sergeant's stripes and an increase in pay. I made sure half my pay increase went straight to Mother, and the other half went to buying War Bonds.

Blythe, California, was a desert air base on the California/Arizona border just west of the Colorado River. The area crawled with rattlesnakes that often lay in ambush outside tents, along walkways, and in latrines. Days got blazing hot, and highs in the 120s were not uncommon. You could boil water on cement, and even in our heavy GI shoes, our feet burned and blistered. At Blythe, we finally found out who could tolerate high altitudes. We were put into a long cylinder with a door at one end and several small round porthole windows on each side. Along both sides were canvas benches, each holding five men. When the men had entered and the door was shut, the attendant on the outside turned a handle, sealing the cylinder. To pass this test you had to be able to spend at least three hours inside as the air was slowly removed until the pressure was equivalent to that experienced at 35,000 feet. Each man was given three chances to pass the test; those who failed were demoted to ground duty. Three men failed, and we tried to make them feel better, not realizing that many of us would not survive the war and that all three of them almost certainly would.

We spent one day learning how to pack a parachute, and from then on I prayed I'd never have to rely on a parachute I packed. Fortunately, in combat, all chutes were packed by experts. We never made any practice parachute jumps; we just watched some films on how to jump from an airplane. Some of us would never need to learn it, and others would either learn fast or die trying. Blythe's training lasted four weeks, and then I reported to Clovis, New Mexico, for flight crew training. Since I'd been trained in a Liberator in San Diego, I was assigned to a B-24 crew.

At Clovis, each member of a crew was prepared for his specific onboard duties. In combat, a flight crew would have to operate as one unified combat team, and this was the first of a three-phase training program that every crew had to go through before the Army Air Force would release you for combat. The B-24 combat crew consisted of 10 men. Four were commissioned officers: the pilot, co-pilot, navigator, and bombardier. The pilot and co-pilot together flew the plane. The navigator kept the plane on course to and from the target, while the bombardier made sure the bombs were released at the correct time. The other six men were non-commissioned officers, sergeants. The first flight engineer was the onboard mechanic and general trouble-shooter, and operated the top turret guns, which would be taken over by the radio operator if problems with the plane required the engineer's attention. The radio operator was stationed directly behind the co-pilot, and the top turret was directly behind the pilot's compartment. The second flight engineer would man one of the .50-caliber waist guns, and the other waist gun would be manned by a second gunner. The waist guns were either side, between the bomb bay and the tail. The tail turret gunner manned the tail guns, protecting the Liberator from attacks from behind, and the ball turret or belly gunner manned the cramped ball turret that was in the bottom of the waist.

After two missions as a trainee flight engineer, I was reassigned to advanced training, and after many hours of classroom lectures and tests I was promoted to instructor of flight engineers and awarded another stripe. As a staff sergeant, and with the extra flight pay, I now made quite a bit more than I had only months earlier. I racked up 150 hours as a flight engineer instructor during that period, the bulk consisting of nerve-wracking takeoffs and landings by novice pilots, almost none of whom had ever flown a four-engine aircraft before. We'd shoot one takeoff and landing after another, six to eight hours a day.

Most crashes occur during takeoff or landing. It's the riskiest part of the flight. Each takeoff and landing had the potential for disaster, and each day seemed like a lifetime. I was responsible for training one new flight engineer every two days.

When I requested combat status, my superiors were surprised, because I would have been able to spend the entire war Stateside as an instructor. My reasoning for leaving what some considered to be a safe posting was that combat could not be any more dangerous than flying with beginner pilots day after day, most of whom acted like they wanted to dive the plane into the runway every time they landed. It was amazing to me how much punishment those planes could take day after day. I remembered at B-24 school they'd taught us that the plane was built like a tank, but I don't think they ever expected the type of abuse the planes were given at Clovis! Sometimes a plane would hit the ground so hard it would bounce back into the air many times before the novice could keep it on the ground. On other occasions, only lightning-fast intervention by the instructor prevented a catastrophic crash. One of my duties as flight engineer was to stand between the pilot and co-pilot and call out the air speed during landings. Many a time all I could do was sweat, close my eyes, and pray.

At Advanced Bomber Training at Pueblo, Colorado, we formed our combat crew. It would be our collective responsibility to mold ourselves into an effective fighting machine. With cooperation, skill, and luck, we could do what was expected of us and come home alive. We had all our crew assigned at this point except for our co-pilot. Five of us were former instructors, and we felt we had a better than average chance of making it through in one piece. I was the youngest of the ten. Though 18, I looked 12. When we entered combat, I was the youngest crewman in the group at 19. The rest were in their twenties and thirties. One of our waist gunners was the old man at 36, which also happened to be the maximum age a man could fly combat. We were from all walks of life and most parts of the U.S. Several men were from Pennsylvania, with one each from Indiana, California, Florida, New York, Connecticut, Massachusetts, and North Carolina.

Thankfully, no one was a medal-happy war-lover. Since every one of our crew was determined to live out the war, we worked together to make that goal possible. Some of the crew balked at first at trusting their lives to such a baby-faced flight engineer, but over time, I earned their respect. The addition of our co-pilot, who'd been training in P-51 Mustang fighters, completed our crew. The co-pilot was disappointed, to say the least, at being reassigned to a heavy bomber but soon became a valuable member of our crew.

Flight crew training was demanding and dangerous. The terrain was mountainous, and we spent a lot of time flying around and dropping dummy bombs. The only training we gunners got was when fighter planes from a nearby base would attack us, checking their gun cameras later to count kills. We gunners would return fire, but without live ammo we never knew if we hit anything. We'd have to learn that in combat.

After a final cross-country training flight to Galveston, Texas, we were given a brief leave, during which we all went our own ways to say one final goodbye to our families and loved ones. Before I knew it I was walking up the hill to our small "house on a hill," and then sadly walking back down and bidding goodbye to Mother and Toby at the station. As the train pulled in, Mother stood at my side and tightly grasped my hand.

I climbed aboard and found my seat, looking at Mother standing alone on the platform. She'd spent her life caring for others, with no regard for herself. Her body was bent from years of scrubbing floors and doing hard physical labor not meant for her small frame. She stood in her homemade dress and apron. Her old shoes had been patched many times and bulged at the toes where overworked feet and improper fit had taken their toll. Her face was creased with wrinkles, her gray hair neatly combed back in a knot at the nape of her neck. On her head, she wore a battered, black-rimmed straw hat with a few faded flowers stuck in its band, but she wore it as proudly as any queen wears a golden crown. Her hands were rough and gnarled from a lifetime of toil. For the first time in my life, I saw signs of sorrow in her face, and I knew that by leaving I was breaking her heart. As the train moved away, I thought of how she'd molded me all these years, just one of her many children. As she grew smaller and smaller in the distance, I prayed that I could be loyal to both my loves—my mother and my country. A ways down the tracks, we passed the very spot where my father's life had ended 17 years before.

Back in Lincoln, the crew waited to find out if we would be sent to the Atlantic Theater or the Pacific. I prayed for the Atlantic because Pacific missions required a lot of over-water flight. A near-drowning in my youth had left me with a fear of water. I was therefore disappointed when we were issued jungle gear and given a gamut of shots that left us feverish and made several of the crew very sick, delaying our departure to the Pacific. While we waited for new orders, our pilot got married. By the time all the crew was well again, the group to which we had been assigned had left without us. Our jungle gear was re-collected and instead we were issued emergency gear for the European Theater. Our crew was assigned a brand-new B-24H bomber to fly to England, made at some plant in Texas, and just like a modern automobile, it had that "new-car smell" when we climbed aboard. On September 26, 1943, we took off with full tanks for Presque Isle, Maine. Since our flight plan would take us within 10 miles of my hometown, our pilot lowered us down to 500 feet and we flew over. It was Sunday morning, and mother was at church, but I could see my dog Toby standing beneath the clothes line, looking up as though he knew it was me.

Each stop on the route to England brought with it new adventures and challenges. The further north we went, the colder it got. The winter clothing, including the sheepskin suits we'd been issued in Lincoln, became more and more appreciated. In addition, each man on the crew had been issued a down sleeping bag. These were doubly appreciated because most of the transit bases had skimpy bedding. Each leg of the voyage traversed hundreds of miles of frigid ocean, and we knew that beneath its blue-green waves German U-boats watched for us, hoping to shoot us down. Survival after a ditching in the North Atlantic was measured in minutes.

The final leg of our flight would take us into England, but included a stretch near Norway, now in German hands. For the first time, we were given the command to test-fire our guns. I pulled the trigger in the top turret, cutting loose two very powerful .50-caliber machine guns. With the gun barrels only inches from either side of my head, the noise was deafening. Seeing the tracer bullets leaving the barrels like a solid flame and watching the shells go through the guns at lightning speed, I knew I had at my command two very powerful weapons.

The emerald coast of Scotland suddenly appeared below through the mist, and our radio operator made contact with the RAF field at Wicks. The field was not built for heavy bombers, but the RAF had landed some heavies there in emergencies and gave us the green light. It was late afternoon, October 14, 1943, when our wheels touched British soil for the first time. We were treated like royalty by the British at the base. All the glory they heaped upon us was unnerving. These men had been fighting the Germans for two years, and here they were honoring us greenhorn Americans fresh in from the States. After a good meal and a good night's sleep, I think we all felt we were ready to continue on and do battle against the Germans.

On October 18 we flew to a replacement sub-depot close to the small village of Baston, only 50 miles from our final destination, the base of the 44th Bomb Group at Shipdham, England, where we became the newest members of the 66th Squadron. Shipdham is located in Norfolk county, just west of Norwich, around 40 miles from the North Sea and directly west of Holland. The 44th Bomb Group was made up of four squadrons—the 66th, the 67th, the 68th, and the 506th. We checked in and were assigned to our Quonset huts, officers in their section, enlisted men in theirs. Each enlisted men's Quonset held 12 men, and with six enlisted men to a crew, this meant two crews per hut. We settled in and located the mess hall, the PX, and the Enlisted Men's Club. We were ready to put our training to the test and do our part to defeat the enemy, and with luck, to stay alive in the process so that we could go home again after the war to our loved ones, and our children could live in peace and freedom.

CHAPTER 2

Combat

Even before we began flying missions with the 44th, the ball turret gunner and I went on a different kind of mission, better known as a double-date. He was new to our crew; our previous gunner shot himself in the foot with his service revolver shortly after our arrival, ostensibly an accident but possibly a way to escape combat. The new ball gunner wanted to make a good impression on me, and since he had been on the base for some time, he already had a steady girlfriend. And *she* had a friend that wanted to meet a Yank, so naturally he thought of me.

We dressed in our natty Air Corps uniforms and I hoped for the best. It was a pitch black, moonless night, but he knew his way around the small village by memory, and we met both girls just outside their homes. I was introduced, and we four made our way to the local pub. I was bashful, unpracticed in the finer art of conversing with the opposite sex, and she must have been the same, although we did hold hands on the way there, mostly so we would not get separated in the inky darkness.

I felt a bit uneasy not being able to see the young lady with whom I was about to make my entrance to the pub, but felt confident that my ball turret gunner wouldn't steer me wrong. I convinced myself that she would be a beautiful blonde English girl like the ones I'd seen so many pictures of. When we entered the pub, I got a shock. My date was at least 30 years my senior, and (forgive me) one of the ugliest women I'd ever seen. One look at my friend, who indeed had one of those beautiful English girls seen in pictures, indicated to me that he shared my surprise. The tiny English pub was packed with rowdy chatting locals drinking beer, playing darts, and eating, but the place went dead quiet upon the entrance of the two uniformed Yanks and their dates, and it seemed every eye was riveted upon me and my blind date. One Englishman nudged me sympathetically as we passed by and said, "Blind date, eh, Yank?" As the night progressed, I found that what the good Lord took from her in looks, he gave back in a wonderful personality, and we ended up having a grand time. When the ball turret gunner and I got back to the barracks, and were faced with the usual questions about the loveliness of my blind date, we both lied and said she'd been gorgeous.

The 44th Bomb Group's base at Shipdham, scraped out of lush East Anglian farmland, was a small city dedicated to one thing—bringing the war to Hitler's Third Reich. In addition to the main runways with control tower, there were miles of taxi strips, dozens of dispersal areas and hardstands for the planes, acres of barracks for the men to live in, a mess hall to eat in, administration buildings, a hospital—essentially everything a small town of 2,000 young American men might need to live and wage war in a faraway land. The base was dispersed over a wide area to prevent Luftwaffe bombs from wiping out more than one plane or building at a time. After evaluating the distances on the base, one of the waist gunners and I bought ourselves a bicycle. Though he was the eldest and I the youngest, we both enjoyed walking and exploring. I also became friends with our plane's crew chief and his crew, and before long I'd cycle out to the hardstand to help with the plane's maintenance when we weren't flying. The ground crews worked long hours at the dispersal points, and didn't have the luxury of a roof under which to work. Even engines were replaced in the cold, damp, rainy English weather. Conditions were often miserable, but they didn't complain. Our crew chief stuttered badly, a fact that embarrassed him. But he was the very best, and did everything possible to keep our beat-up planes airworthy.

We made a few training flights around England, learning the topography and adjusting to the weather, which was generally cloudy or foggy and not nearly as ideal as it had been back in training in the States. We were also given more ground schooling. Conditions were much more hazardous in England, with the poor visibility and the great number of planes in the air at a time. Often, there were hundreds of planes flying around in the same air space, in clouds so thick you couldn't see the plane in front of you. Midair collisions were common, usually with few survivors.

The English winter of 1943–44 was one of the worst in decades, clouds and fog all but shutting down combat missions for days or weeks at a time. The delays were hard on all of us. Our crew arrived at the 44th on October 21, 1943 and didn't fly our first mission until January 11, 1944. That's a long time to sit around and anticipate combat! As strange as it may seem, everyone was anxious to get that first combat mission under his belt. No one can tell you what combat is like; you have to experience it for yourself. Only then would each of us know if we had what it took to overcome our fears and perform our duties. My biggest fear was never the enemy—it was the fear of letting down my crew and my country.

Before we flew combat as a crew, our pilot flew a combat mission as co-pilot with an experienced crew to give him a feel for it. That crew was short a waist gunner, so one of ours went too. While our two friends were gone, the rest of us spent an anxious day "sweating out the mission," worrying for our two crew members. We'd come so far with our pilot, and to lose him now would be devastating. We had complete trust in his ability and felt there could be no better person. We literally trusted him with our lives. He would prove worthy of this trust time and again, both in combat and after we were interned.

Back in Lincoln, all 10 crewmen were issued two-layered heavy-weather clothing. The outer layer consisted of a jacket and pants made of heavy sheep skin and also included gloves, boots, and a helmet. The inner layer was an electrically heated flight suit, sometimes called a "bunny suit," that looked and functioned much like an electric blanket. It was wired for heat, and once the terminals were fastened together and the suit was plugged in, the wires warmed up and kept you comfortable at high altitudes in the unheated, unpressurized B-24, where temperatures could easily plunge to minus-60 degrees Fahrenheit. The suits worked great in theory, but poorly in combat. We either roasted or froze with them. The spots where your body bent at the elbows or knees overheated. When we'd arrived at the sub-depot in England we'd lost not only our brand-new plane, but also our new heated flying suits. From then on, we'd get issued electric suits from the equipment room before each mission, and wearing someone else's smelly, sweaty suit was similar to wearing someone else's underwear.

It seems strange that perhaps the pivotal event of our crew's experience in England involved something as mundane as sleeping bags, but it did. These sleeping bags almost got our entire crew killed. When we were issued our cold-weather gear in Lincoln, we'd also each been issued a high-quality, heavy-duty sleeping bag. The Air Corps had just started issuing these to all crewmembers; before, the bags had only been issued to officers. Our sleeping bags quickly became the envy of every man who had arrived before the rule change, but we were allowed to keep them per new regulation. One day shortly after our arrival, our enlisted men's hut was inspected by the base operations officer, a major in charge of all the squadron's crews. When we returned from the practice mission, we were floored to find our sleeping bags had been taken away, confiscated by the operations officer to be redistributed to officers. We found out later that this actually meant the operations officer and his friends. To make matters worse, many of us had placed our wallets in the foot of our bags and these were also gone. To rub salt into the wound, the other crew in our hut had been envious of our sleeping bags and took great delight in letting us know that we now had to join the "common folks" and freeze like everybody else under a single thin, GI-issued wool blanket.

As the first flight engineer, I was in charge of the enlisted crew. If it had been up to me I would have dropped the whole thing. The radio operator, who was the same rank as me and 14 years my senior, was a hot-blooded Italian-American who took nothing from nobody. We discussed what, if anything, we could do about this injustice. After much debate, his faction won and it was decided we would advocate for our rights and try to get our sleeping bags back. We discussed this with our pilot, who along with the other officers had not lost his bag, and he said he'd back our cause.

We got our bags back, and we also got something else. From then on, we were assigned the worst available plane in the squadron on every single mission, and assigned to fly it in the worst possible position in the formation—coffin corner. The operations officer probably figured we'd last a few missions, we'd get shot down, and that he could have our bags. A pretty petty reason to send men to their deaths. Men were probably killed over much less a thousand times during the war.

CHAPTER 3

Missions

It was decided our crew was as good as could be expected and was now ready to fly combat over Germany. The sleeping bag issue hurt our poor ground chief and his small crew as well. They were responsible for making sure every rattle-trap crate assigned to us got us there and back, and believe me, these planes were some of the worst specimens in the entire Eighth Air Force. They did a remarkable job.

As I prepared to fly combat, I pondered my pacifist Quaker upbringing. The only living thing I'd killed up to that time was a rabbit to feed my family, and I had no idea what I'd do in the moment when I was confronted with the dilemma of "Kill or Be Killed"—a saying posted on signs all over our base. Perhaps I joined the Air Force as a way not to have to see those I killed, knowing I'd be flying thousands of feet above the enemy. Even so, I would find that I got a sick feeling every time we dropped our bombs and I watched them exploding in the German cities below, walking their way across city streets, churches, train stations, parks, and shopping districts. I got the same sick feeling every time an enemy plane exploded before my eyes after my bullets tore through it. I never took credit for hitting an enemy plane, hoping, I suppose, that it had been shot down by bullets from another gunner on my plane or on another B-24, even when deep down I knew I was the only one shooting. It wasn't until after the war that I realized that I and millions of other young men had been fooling themselves. If the Bible is true, then I find it very hard to believe that there is a place in heaven for us. Black is black and white is white. Killing is killing. Madmen make excuses for us to kill, but that doesn't relieve us from culpability. I can only pray that there is some place besides heaven for those of us who killed others, believing we were doing the right thing. Even though I feel this way, I also feel it was my duty to fight oppression. It was a moral and an ethical dilemma that was beyond me then and remains beyond me to this day. It has caused me, in the decades since the war, to feel a continuous vacuum every time I pray to my God.

Paradoxically, I must further admit that I felt great excitement each time we were rousted out in the wee hours of the morning, waking up long before daybreak, checking out our flight suits and equipment, and going to the briefing room to find out where we'd be flying that day. It was an indescribable feeling, a feeling of being wholly and totally alive and aware, perhaps because we knew some of us would be dead before the day was over and we were reveling in every moment, every sight and smell and sound. As we trudged out to our planes, there was a feeling of closeness and kinship that one will never experience in civilian life. Perhaps that is why war is so popular—this feeling one gets when one goes through the fiery crucible with men who become so much closer than blood brothers.

Thanks to our friendly operations officer, our first plane looked like one of the Dog Patch airliners in the *Lil' Abner* comic strip popular at the time. The plane had more patches than original skin, the tires were worn bald, and the metal around the engine nacelles and the wing behind each was covered with a thick sludge of caked-on engine oil. The landing struts and nose wheel wept hydraulic strut oil which dribbled in a steady stream out of the worn-out seals on the landing struts and the nose wheel. We looked at the plane in dismay, unwilling to believe that this deathtrap was capable of leaving the ground empty, let alone packed with tons of bombs and fuel. Surviving mission one looked doubtful. However, our highly skilled ground crew had made sure that every vital mechanical part worked. When we pre-flighted the engines, they checked out within acceptable limits.

The threats of our operations officer began to take on an even more sinister significance. In the 66th Squadron, each pilot was given the option to refuse to fly a plane if he thought it was not safe after it had been checked for the day's mission. For some reason, our pilot was never given this option; instead, it was up to our ground crew and me to make the necessary repairs before takeoff. In 25 missions, we never aborted because of mechanical problems, though many other crews did. We were as determined to come back from each mission as our bastard operations officer was to make sure we didn't. To do so, we spent many hours scavenging in the base "boneyard," harvesting spare parts. The B-24, contrary to what many have said and written about it, was a remarkably durable plane. No matter what shape it was in or what damage it took, the plane could do wonders fighting off the enemy and returning to base.

On January 11, 1944, we finally flew our first mission. For the first 17 missions, we flew coffin corner in the worst planes the operations officer could find. Each mission was a trip to hell and back, and we never knew when we climbed aboard at the beginning of the day if we would live to see the sun go down. The old saying about flak is that it got so thick you could walk on it, and this was certainly true on many of our missions. The black smoke from exploding shells looked frightening, but the thousands of shards of jagged shrapnel flying through the air and the concussion from the explosion were the real killers. During each flak explosion, a plane could pick up dozens of holes. Some entered the plane with little damage, but other fragments hit fuel cells, or their connecting lines to the engines, or destroyed other critical parts. And the concussion of a German .88mm shell was even more damaging in the air than on the ground. When a shell detonated close enough, the concussion could take down three or four planes. There were times when a flak burst would tear a plane's wing off or completely turn a plane over. If a crew was lucky, some men might have time to jump out before the plane's death fall. When we saw any plane in our group explode, whether we knew the crew personally or not, it was a horrific psychological blow. Sometimes, a plane and its crewmen simply vanished in an oily smudge. At other times, we would follow the pieces of the plane downward, praying for parachutes to open, hoping that at least one man would get out alive.

Sometimes they did. Sometimes they didn't.

Watching men die damages your heart and soul. It also drove home the point, made in training, that we were expendable. In one Stateside training class, a crewman had commented that if a B-24 and its highly trained 10-man crew were to go down on its first mission, it would be a huge loss for the Air Corps. The instructor replied, with a straight face, that the plane and crew was only a loss if it had failed to drop its bombs on the target. "If the crew on its one and only mission puts their bombs on the target," he blandly informed us, "the Army Air Force considers the plane and crew fully paid for."

The more important the target, the more opposition the Germans threw at us. First it would be fighters, and then the fighters would move out of range and radio the formation's exact altitude and speed to the flak guns on the ground, and they would take over. We did what we could to confuse their radar, dropping shredded aluminum foil strips, called chaff, but that didn't protect us from fighters calling us in. Even when the resistance was light, we expected the worst, and tensions remained high. Flying at 25,000 feet during the winter months, temperatures were 40 to 60 degrees below zero Fahrenheit. And wearing that tight-fitting oxygen mask for eight hours, inhaling sub-zero oxygen, made a man claustrophobic and a little crazy.

We expected a milk run—an easy break-in mission—on our first combat sortie, but had no such luck. Instead, we went to one of the most fortified targets in northern Germany. Our group split in two and hit two different targets that day. One was a submarine base on the North Sea, using blockbuster bombs to try to penetrate the 12-foot-thick concrete U-boat bunkers. Our squadron ventured deeper into Germany and hit a fighter factory. Seeing the enemy fighters coming at us out of the sun head on, spinning through the squadron, taking out several bombers, gave me my first feeling of absolute terror. All the schooling on ballistics—on sighting through the gun rings, figuring distance, calculating speed in order to lead the target—was a waste of time in combat. Each fighter came and went so fast I never seemed to have time to sight in on one. The first few fighters that blazed through our formation, I watched spellbound. By the time I snapped out of it and tried to line the fighter up in my sights, it would be gone before I could squeeze off a single round. Finally, our pilot came on the interphone and calmly asked me, "Culler, that was the enemy that just passed through. Surely you saw them. Aren't you going to shoot?"

I was feeling mighty low for letting the crew down, and the next time a group of four white-nosed Me109s attacked, guns blazing, I pulled the trigger, so engrossed in the sight of my tracers stitching toward them that I forgot to let up. I blasted long after the fighters were gone. In that one continuous burst, I'd used up half my ammunition! The pilot's not-so-calm voice came on the interphone again: "For God's sake, Culler, let off!" In my first contact with the enemy, I'd frozen and not fired and then frozen and emptied half my ammo. My heart pounding like a jackhammer, sweat rolling down my forehead and clogging my goggles, I was beginning to have some serious doubts about my readiness for combat.

A few minutes later, another wave of German fighters came through our formation, and I managed to squeeze off some well-placed short bursts into the enemy. Again, my pilot's voice crackled through my headphones. "Good job, Dan." Maybe there was hope! Maybe now I would be a credit to the crew and the squadron. We went on to the target, dropped our bombs, and headed back to England, and I tried to block out the fact that our bombs had killed other human beings, telling myself that only steel and concrete were being destroyed. We returned to England in terrible weather. Our wheels chirped against the concrete runway and we taxied to our dispersal area. Our crew chief and his crew were there, waving, smiling wide proud smiles. We climbed out of the plane with a sense of pride and accomplishment—we'd flown the worst plane in the squadron, in the coffin corner, overcome our first-mission jitters, and except for a few flak holes, returned with crew and aircraft in one piece.

Weeks passed, and we targeted many different places in Germany. Most were factories making war equipment, such as aircraft plants, ball-bearing plants, and refineries. Many sites were along the Rhine River. The missions began to add up. We needed 25 to be done and go home. However, there were worrying rumors that the 8th Air Force was planning to increase the number of required missions from 25 to 30. If this were true, we felt that the only way we'd return to the States was in a pine box. Another rumor making the rounds was that the higher-ups were sending every man who completed the magic 25 missions to training schools back in the States where they would be transitioned over into the brand new B-29 bomber and then sent to bomb Japan. I made up my mind that if I completed my 25, I would volunteer to stay in Europe and fly missions, rather than fly thousands of miles over the Pacific. I found the Pacific much scarier than German flak or fighters.

On March 6, 1944, our group participated in the first large-scale daylight bombing mission of Berlin. The Berlin mission was momentous for our crew in another way; it was the first mission we were given our very own B-24, a newer B-24H. We proudly named her "Hell's Kitten," and our crew chief polished her until she shined.

Over the course of our missions, we flew so deep into Germany that if we lost more than 200 gallons of fuel to headwinds or a fuel tank puncture, there was no way we could make it back to England. With Europe under occupation, any landing on the continent meant likely imprisonment unless a crew could make it to Sweden or Switzerland. I was proud to be a part of the 8th Air Force, which had proven the pundits wrong in thinking daylight precision bombing would fail. The losses we took would be unacceptable today, but we stayed determined, and each month, it seemed that there were fewer enemy aircraft opposing us. No matter how many the Germans sent up, we had been as successful in destroying the Luftwaffe, in the air and on the ground, and even on the assembly lines, as they had been in destroying so many of our own aircraft in 1942 and 1943.

Our new B-24H Liberator, "Hell's Kitten," became ours exclusively on our twentieth mission. Though it was one of the older planes in the squadron, you could actually see smooth aluminum skin without patches upon patches. Patches cost an airplane as much as 20 miles per hour in air speed. The engines looked like they didn't leak much oil, and the inside didn't look like it had been used in a shooting gallery. Our new plane was also eye-catching. It was the first in the squadron to have a name and artwork on both sides of the nose. The painting of a beautiful, scantily clad woman between the "Hell's" and the "Kitten" was sure to bring us luck. It had likely been painted on by the crew who had flown her to England, on the mistaken assumption that she would be theirs.

I did have one concern about our new plane. During the March 6 Berlin mission, my top turret had failed to work above 18,000 feet. This turret was my combat position and defended our aircraft from attacks from above. It used an electrical control mechanism that rotated the turret and moved the gun up and down, but this mechanism would not work. The trigger worked, so at least the gun operated. I'd reported it after we got back, but it malfunctioned again on our second mission to Berlin on March 8.

Without the turret's normal mechanism, I was forced to handcrank the turret to rotate it—a terrible way to try to track a fast-moving target and shoot at it at the same time. Other crews in the squadron reported on the mission that the top turret wasn't tracking and shooting. I was told to get it fixed, and I tried, but every time I got it back, it still didn't work. Other crews would say, "Get it fixed or refuse to fly." Easier said than done, unfortunately. No matter how much I complained, it never got fixed. The armory officer would look at it and tell me that they'd checked it out on the ground and it worked fine, and that there was nothing in the mechanism of the turret that should cause it to fail at higher altitudes. The armory officer even hinted that I was developing a yellow streak up my back, which angered my crew chief to the point that angry words were exchanged. I then suggested the armory officer take the plane up to 18,000 feet and test it for himself. He rejected this suggestion indignantly, reminding me he was not paid to fly but that I was, and that if I didn't shut up I'd be grounded and lose my stripes. I continued to write it up for repair after every mission, but nothing was done.

We were in line to become a lead crew in the 66th Squadron, meaning advancement in rank for our officers, so it was important that we performed our best. The top turret was a bugaboo. Our pilot decided that I could operate it fairly well by hand and elected to keep the plane and not make waves. The other gunners, especially the nose and tail gunners, would try to protect my firing zone if I were slow to respond. We failed to realize that German fighter pilots were adept at spotting weaknesses in a bomber formation and exploiting them. Many times, when our own fighters weren't around, a lone German fighter would follow us, just out of range, and observe our firing power. He couldn't help but notice the slowness of the top turret.

We were over a very long, well-fortified target in lower Germany when we came under heavy fighter attack. I could hear the other members of the crew barking out directions until our pilot told us to remember to talk one at a time. I cranked my turret toward the rear and saw fighters attacking from behind. Our tail gunner blasted them as they spun down below the formation. Coming up from the rear was something new for the German fighters. It eliminated our deadly waist gunners from the equation, and it meant they only had to deal with the tail and ball gunners. From this position, the fighters were able to fire their shells directly into the underside of the wings of our bombers, ripping through our gas tanks and causing an explosion.

A German Me109 appeared out of nowhere, a short distance behind our plane. It was climbing, and its belly filled my gun sight, hanging there for what seemed forever, but was probably no more than a second. At first it startled me, and it must have startled the tail gunner, too, because for that long moment, neither of us fired. Then we both came to our senses and unloaded our guns into the belly of the German plane, at the center of the wing area, sending our shells ripping into the armor plating protecting its fuel tanks. No plating on earth could withstand that assault, and the plane exploded into pieces, fragments, both large and small, showering out in all directions.

A large section of the German fighter's wing fluttered slowly and deliberately through the pale blue sky, turning end over end, almost in slow motion. Another bomber flew just to one side of us, less than a hundred feet away, and the wing struck the bomber hard, slicing into it. As we watched in horror, the bomber's own wing broke away from the fuselage, and both plane and wing began their death plunge to the earth thousands of feet below. As it tumbled like a leaf, we prayed for parachutes, but saw none.

As the fog of battle cleared, I realized I had just helped bring down one of our own aircraft. I knew the crew. One of my best friends was the flight engineer. We'd exchanged addresses, and I wrote his mother after the war, hoping he might have made it out of the plane and become a prisoner of war. She wrote back that, no, he had been shot down on a mission and killed over Germany.

After we returned to Shipdham, at the debriefing, neither the tail gunner nor myself mentioned shooting down the German fighter. In fact, we never mentioned it to anyone, or even talked about it between ourselves. It was as if it never happened, and I guess if you want to keep your sanity, this is the way you have to do it. We were the only two who saw what happened. That damn near killed me. I have never gotten over the fact that in addition to killing the German pilot, I'd killed my closest friend and his crew.

We had one more mission, number 25, after which I would have done my duty to my nation. On the way back from 24, I was beginning to rethink my decision about signing up again. How far can one press one's luck? Although I'd told the new operations officer I would sign on for five more, I wasn't yet committed. My friends thought I was crazy for even considering it, not aware that my fear of ocean flying was the root cause, not foolhardiness or courage.

Mission 25 loomed, the final obstacle.

CHAPTER 4

Shot Down and Internment Camp

On the morning of our 25th and final mission, everyone got up hoping for a milk run. We'd never had a milk run; in fact, some of our worst missions were short ones. We'd learned not to count on the Germans making any of our missions easy.

Weather was our enemy, too. Several of us suffered from frozen feet. This was endemic on the base due to a shortage of heated flight suits. It had become so serious that, several weeks before, our flight surgeon had threatened to ground the entire squadron unless enough heated flight suits could be procured. This was a problem on other bases as well. There was a story making the rounds that a flight surgeon had driven his Jeep out to the end of the runway before a mission, preventing his squadron from taking off until they had enough working flight suits. He was finally removed by MPs, but when the squadron returned, bearing many men with frostbite, a plane had flown in with enough brand-new heated flight suits for everyone.

I woke up early that morning, before we were even rousted out. The old waist gunner and I rode our bikes to the mess hall and stuffed ourselves with what we jokingly referred to as "our last meal." It was March 18, 1944, only four days before my twentieth birthday. It was a bone-chilling morning, even for England this time of year. The briefing hut was packed, all eyes fixed on the curtain on the stage, eager to see where we'd be flying, so that we could begin figuring our odds of coming home. When the curtain was pulled, deep groans filled the

34 • PRISONER OF THE SWISS

room. This wouldn't be an easy one. We were flying to Friedrichshafen to bomb a large ball-bearing plant on the western side of the city on the shores of Lake Constance. The target area was highly fortified to protect the German steel mills along the lake that used the lake water in the steel-making process. The great distance from our base meant there would be little margin for error on fuel. In fact, if there was a strong headwind either way, or if our fuel lines were to get damaged, return would be unlikely.

To make matters worse, we could only attack and leave from one direction, because the southern half of Lake Constance was in Switzerland, a neutral country. We were warned that if we crossed the thin line between Germany and Switzerland Swiss fighters and antiaircraft would open up on us. The Swiss used German weapons and aircraft, and we had no doubts that they were as lethal as the Germans, though perhaps not as battle-trained.

Today our crew would fly as group leader, carrying a special radar bombsight that allowed us to bomb through clouds or overcast. The rest of the group would bomb on our command. We were proud of this, and so was our ground crew. Despite flying the worst planes in the squadron, we had never aborted a mission, and now we were flying lead. As we climbed aboard, our trusty crew chief bid us goodbye with the words, "Give 'em hell and we'll see you tonight."

We taxied out of our dispersal area and along the taxi strip, each plane falling in behind us as we headed for the main runway. We hurtled down the runway, and finally the four powerful engines lifted us inch by inch into the air, followed at intervals by the rest of the squadron, and we climbed into the English sky as we had so many times before. It was an all-out effort; the entire U.S. Eighth Air Force was going to bomb Germany somewhere today. Every American fighter was flying in support, charged with protecting the bomber stream and then "hitting the deck" with leftover ammunition and strafing German ground targets. The fighters would take off from England long after we did, not only because they flew twice as fast, but because they didn't have to do the endless circling climb to altitude. Rendezvous was set up well down the route, and each fighter group would meet a particular squadron of

4. SHOT DOWN AND INTERNMENT CAMP • 35

bombers. As one fighter group got low on fuel, it would be replaced by another. On this mission, the original fighters would have time to return to base, refuel, and greet us toward the end of our mission.

We climbed higher through the murk, keeping our eyes open for the hundreds of other bombers that also climbed invisibly all around us, and finally leveled off above the clouds, where we waited for our squadron to assemble. Four more planes finally popped up out of the clouds, but they were from another squadron, so they banked away and headed off in search of their own. Our pilot was getting edgy. It seemed nothing was going right. This was a long mission, and every drop of gas was needed. We didn't have any to waste circling around waiting for stragglers. Finally we formed up and headed out over the southern part of the North Sea. When I went to check our fuel and transfer from the auxiliary tank to the main tank, I was concerned to see how much fuel we'd already used.

As usual, we flew in a different direction than our mission object–ive to confuse German fighters. We picked up a lot of flak over the southern Dutch coast. It was never a good thing to get hit by flak this early in a long mission, and soon we saw some of our planes turning back to England, either from flak damage or mechanical malfunction. Every plane that turned around meant less guns defending us from the enemy later.

It was strange to be out in the very front of the entire formation, nothing in front of us but empty sky. When I looked back from my top turret, hundreds of B-24s bobbed up and down in our wake, a veritable armada, the morning sun glinting off their silvery fuselages. With so many planes behind us, I figured our rear was covered, so I cranked my broken turret around to the front.

As expected, we were soon hit by swarming German fighters, engaged by our own fighter escort, and we watched the dogfights between, above, and below us. It was hazy, with scattered clouds, and below us, the German mountains and countryside were blanketed by snow. As we approached the target, the flak became heavy and accurate. As we lined up for the bombing run, we were also hit by buffeting turbulence that shook the plane in all directions. The pilot transferred control of the aircraft to autopilot, and the bombardier was now flying the plane during the bomb run and would drop the bombs using the Norden sight, if clear, or the radar, if not. Between the flak and the turbulence, I don't know how our bombardier was able to keep the bombsight lined up on the target, but he managed. Time slowed down as flak exploded outside our plane, pieces of jagged metal rattling like hail off the plane's thin skin. The bombardier waited for the moment when he could release the bombs, and we waited breathlessly as well.

Suddenly, we were pummeled by an intense explosion under our left wing. As the plane rocked and righted itself, I staggered back to see gasoline pouring in buckets out of the left wing tanks.

"Flames are coming out of the left inboard engine!" our waist gunner yelled over the interphone, and made a move to jump out the waist window. The older waist gunner restrained him, reminding him that he wasn't wearing his parachute. No matter how much our pilot must have longed to take the controls back from the bombardier, he had to wait until after "bombs away." Every plane in the formation was depending on us to drop our bombs correctly. We were the only plane equipped with radar for bombing accuracy, and if we aborted the bomb run, the mission would be wasted. Even though the plane was now veering alarmingly to the left, the bombardier was able to pull it back on course using the bomb sight. Finally, the target appeared in his crosshairs, he pressed the button releasing the bombs, the bombs dropped from the bomb bay, our plane lurched upwards in sudden lightness, and the bombs screamed downward toward the ball-bearing plant.

The rest of the group dropped upon our release and in a split second the sky below was black with bombs. Our pilot now yanked the control wheel over to the left to escape the flak, then banked even tighter so that we were looking down on the middle of Lake Constance, the border between Switzerland and Germany. The waist gunners reported that the fire had gone out but gasoline was streaming from our wing tanks. I got an oxygen bottle and walked back to try to drain the fuel out of the left wing tank into the right tank. The pilot announced that everyone needed to put on his parachute and be prepared to bail out if the plane exploded. Wearing my portable oxygen unit, carrying my parachute, I carefully crossed the narrow 4-inch catwalk through the bomb bay, the

4. SHOT DOWN AND INTERNMENT CAMP • 37

only thing between me and the earth 25,000 feet below. If I fell I would probably be unable to snap my chute on. Halfway across, I could see we were in mortal danger. The pungent reek of gasoline filled the bomb bay, permeating through my oxygen mask, and gas seeped through the rivets between the wing tanks and the bomb bay. I made it across and began pumping gas out of the left tank into the right. Finally the leak began to slow, and it appeared we might not explode in a giant fireball.

The pilot struggled to keep the engines firing while I transferred the fuel. The oil pressure was dropping, and both engines were overheating, even with the engine cowl flaps wide open. He decided we had to drop out of the formation, and the number two plane moved up to take our place. I figured that flak had cut our oil lines and the engines were not getting enough lubrication. It was only a matter of time before each engine seized up.

During our briefings in England, we'd been told that if any plane became too damaged to make it back to England, or if a plane was too low on fuel to get home, and if the plane was close to the Swiss border, then the best course of action was to divert to Switzerland. This would prevent the recovery of the aircraft by the enemy, and would keep the crew out of German prison camps. Switzerland began to look like an option.

We were flying away from the Swiss/German border. The drag on our aircraft was intense, our air speed was dropping, our group was already a formation of small black dots miles ahead of us, and we were losing altitude at an alarming rate. We were all alone, somewhere over southern Germany, and the mountains that had seemed so unthreatening at high altitude now loomed menacingly in our path. It was now or never. The pilot's voice crackled over the interphone, asking the navigator for the quickest route to Switzerland.

As I made my way back to the waist area to reassess our damage, four German Me109 fighters bobbed on the air currents nearby, two on either side. To our relief, the fighters did not open up on us, and our gunners held their fire. These fighters had the white cross of Switzerland marking their sides, something the Swiss pilots were careful to make sure we saw.

38 • PRISONER OF THE SWISS

The gunners left their firing positions, and we put on parachutes in case the pilot gave us the order to bail out. We were surrounded by mountains, and our plane was dying. The only question now was whether we would jump or whether we could land safely.

The pilot came on the interphone. "I've been told by the Swiss pilot that they are escorting us to a Swiss landing strip. We're lowering the gear and going to one-quarter flaps so that we won't be able to abort. Not sure why they think we'll do that, 1,000 miles from our lines and with two bad engines, but there you have it. Culler, get ready to destroy the plane if we are able to land safely."

While I destroyed the plane, the bombardier would put a bullet through the Norden bombsight to prevent it from falling into enemy hands. The radio man had already disabled our radio so the Germans wouldn't be able to receive and transmit messages, and he was in the process of tearing up his code book into small pieces. I helped him throw the scraps out the window.

Assuming we made a safe landing, my plan was to run back to the waist gunner's position and hide above the wing section at the fuel transfer station where all the large fuel lines were exposed, then cut the lines, switch on the pump, and set the plane on fire using a flare gun once the crew was clear of the plane.

We touched down, instantly pulled to one side by a flat tire, and I was nearly thrown from the plane. I made it to the wing section and pulled out my small, rusty pocket knife. The gunners bailed out of the plane as fast as they could, the pilot gave me the "All clear!" and I began sawing my way through the fuel line, but it was like cutting through steel with a butter knife. When we landed, the hard landing had twisted the metal to the point where the huge wing fuel tanks ruptured. It's a miracle we weren't blown sky-high. I jumped from the wing and ran to the catwalk, flare gun in hand, planning to shoot the flare into the gas streaming from the wing tank once I was clear. Before I could jump from the bomb bay, my leg was caught in a firm grip and I was dragged roughly from the plane. A large body flattened out on top of me and a hand wrestled the flare gun from me just as my finger pulled the trigger. The gun failed to fire, probably saving both our lives. I was covered in gasoline, and if the plane had gone up, I would have gone up with it, along with the Swiss soldier and probably many others.

Three Swiss soldiers surrounded me, and a gun was pointed at my head. We were one of 13 Allied crews who diverted to Switzerland that day. Some bailed out before their planes exploded in fireballs against the walls of mountains. Others made it to the airport shot up and in bad shape. One B-17 struggled in on one engine, and several others made belly landings, their gear shot up. We landed with 90 gallons of fuel left, not enough to have made a go-round for a second approach.

CHAPTER 5

Interned at Adelboden

Our crew and several others were taken under Swiss guard to a large theater similar to our briefing room back in England, and were given a form to fill out with our name and other personal information. We'd been trained in the general points of the Geneva Convention, which stipulates a prisoner has only to give his name, rank, and serial number; however, we were then told that the Geneva Convention didn't apply because we weren't prisoners and in any case Switzerland was not a signatory. This information was given to us by a tall, blond Swiss officer who seemed the embodiment of the Nazi Aryan ideal seen on posters and in movies. He was cocky and sarcastic in his demeanor and comments. Also up front was the American military attaché to Switzerland, Brigadier General Barnwell Legge. Legge, dressed in a World War I vintage cavalry uniform with jodhpurs, spoke to us in a tone suggesting he held us in low regard, at roughly the level of scum or traitors. He informed us that we were internees, not prisoners, and commanded us not to escape. This went directly against everything we had been taught in our training, which was that if we were captured we were to do everything in our power to escape and return to our units. He told us that anyone attempting escape would be harshly dealt with by the Swiss, and that he would do nothing to assist any American soldier who tried it.

As he spoke, I was uncomfortably aware of the fact that my flight suit was saturated with aviation fuel. My skin burned from it. Raising the

5. INTERNED AT ADELBODEN • 41

level of my discomfort was the fact that some of the other men were casually smoking cigarettes. I tried to keep as much distance between the smokers and me as possible to prevent an explosion. To add to my woes, my frost-bitten feet throbbed with pain; later, when I took my flight boots off, I found that the skin on my toes and on the outside of my feet was turning black.

After debriefing, we were taken to a train station and loaded on a train to a small village called Frutigen. At Frutigen, we boarded a bus, which wound its way up a narrow, twisting road high into the Swiss Alps. The higher the bus climbed, and the more our ears popped, the more it sunk in that this was probably the only road to wherever it was we were going. When it seemed we could climb no higher, we reached the small resort village of Adelboden. Adelboden was completely isolated, cut off from civilization by steep, snow-capped mountains. It might as well have had a hundred-foot wall around it and been guarded by an entire army of guards.

Adelboden had been a popular ski resort before the war. Business had nearly ceased once the war started, and the hotels were converted for use by internees. Some American crews were already there, as well as a contingent of British soldiers who had been on an amazing odyssey. Most had been captured by Germany in North Africa, then moved to prison camps in Italy staffed by Italian guards. When Italy quit the war, many of the guards deserted their posts, allowing the Brits to escape before the Germans were able to move in and take command. The Brits made their way northward to Switzerland, where they were interned.

We soon found ourselves living a strange day-to-day existence. Where days before we faced death in hostile skies, we now lived in a resort hotel in the Swiss Alps, albeit a stripped down one. We weren't prisoners in the strictest sense of the word, but we weren't allowed to leave our new mountaintop home either. We were like animals in a beautiful enclosure, with only the illusion of freedom. We could walk the streets, hike the meadows, ride bikes, even ski in season, in our lovely prison. The British and American governments paid the Swiss for our incarceration, even providing us with a small allowance.

Switzerland suffered a food shortage, and food was severely rationed. This was passed on to the internees. We got enough to eat, but nothing more and nothing fancy. The pain in my feet was alleviated somewhat by soaking them in cold water, and I walked every chance I got. My frequent hikes convinced me that unless a man was an expert skier or mountain climber, any escape attempt would end in death.

The same craggy mountains that held us in also kept Germany from invading, I was told. Another reason was Switzerland's lack of natural resources, other than hydroelectric power. Had Germany wanted to conquer Switzerland, I'm convinced it wouldn't have had much of a problem. I was told by one of the guards that 60 percent of the Swiss population was of German or Austrian descent, and many in this part of Switzerland belonged to the Swiss Nazi Party, which was not considerably different from the German party. Maybe this is the reason why we American internees were not looked upon favorably by some townspeople.

The urban Swiss were well-educated. Most spoke several languages, including English. Even in Adelboden, some Swiss offered language classes to the internees. I took French, with the hopes that I could use it to help my eventual escape. Adelboden's few tourists seemed to come primarily to gawk at the American and British prisoners. I got to know one Swiss family from Lucerne, husband and wife and their three daughters. The youngest, who was 17, enjoyed practicing her English with me, as I probably seemed about her own age. I'd heard that if you made friends with a Swiss family and were invited to go to their city for a visit, you could be given a three-day pass, and this provided me with additional motivation to befriend the family. Sure enough, I was invited to visit them in Lucerne, and Adelboden's Swiss commander approved the request. During my visit, I decided that escaping would be damaging to the father's career, and I decided against it.

My next plan was to escape into Italy and join up with the advancing Allied army as it fought its way up Italy's boot. I'd take the bus to Frutigen, board a train to Lucerne, then transfer to another train heading south to Bellinzona, the largest city in southern Switzerland and one that was very close to the Italian border. I mentioned my plan to our ball turret gunner and was surprised when he expressed interest. He in turn had been planning an escape with a British soldier, who had made contact with an Italian family during his escape from Italy to Switzerland. This family was only 5 miles from the Swiss/Italian border, and would let him hide in their barn until the Allies arrived. We decided to team up and escape together.

We each purchased a traditional black wide-brimmed hat, the kind that the Swiss mountain people wore, and got enough money for a round-trip ticket to Bellinzona. Once we reached Bellinzona, we'd strike out into the mountains and walk over the pass into Italy.

CHAPTER 6

The First Escape

The sun had not even broken the mountain peaks when we slipped silently from our rooms and took a circuitous back route to the bus station. The bus always arrived the night before, discharged passengers, and then the driver stayed the night before making the morning's return trip. As we arrived, he was busy fussing over the bus's methane burner, and was pleased to add three more passengers to his roster. The other passengers were workers, and we pretended to be sleeping to avoid conversation, since none of us knew German.

The bus crawled down the mountain on the narrow, winding road, picking up additional passengers at farms and villages along the way. The rustic chalets and quaint mountainside villages looked like pictures in books or on calendars I'd seen as a boy. The bus took us straight to Frutigen's train station. We had a few nervous moments when we recognized a few of our Adelboden guards, but they didn't recognize us, and we bought out tickets to Zurich and Bellinzona without incident.

The train ran through tunnels and along steep mountainsides with precipitous drops, occasionally paralleling the beds of rivers that sparkled in the late morning light. The Zurich train station was bright, beautiful, and clean, and very large. We boarded the train for Bellinzona with no problems. Several people tried to engage us in conversation, and we smiled and nodded. At one stop, a large contingent of Swiss soldiers boarded, wedging into our car with their packs and rifles, filling the coach, even standing in the aisles. The next hour was mighty uncomfortable. The

6. THE FIRST ESCAPE • 45

soldiers kept talking to us in German, and it soon became apparent that we would need a strategy to avoid being found out. I suggested that we pretend to be mutes. We spent the rest of the voyage inventing phony hand signals and having totally meaningless conversations with each other.

Bellinzona had a large station about the size of Zurich's. I figured if we were going to have any trouble during the escape, it would be here; Bellinzona was the largest city on the Italian border, only 20 miles away as the crow flies. We set out from the train station. The weather was cooperating. It was a beautiful day. The sun was out and the sky was a clear, pale blue. We headed south, toward Italy, armed with our small compass.

Bellinzona, it turned out, was also a key area for smuggling goods over the Swiss/Italian border, and the authorities had eyes everywhere. Residents of the area were dark-skinned and looked Italian; the fair-skinned British officer and I stuck out like sore thumbs, and were the subject of many suspicious stares.

For the first time since leaving Adelboden, we were completely on our own, without public transportation. Bellinzona was surrounded by high mountains, and the closer we got to them, the bigger, higher, and more frightening they loomed, especially as the sun began to set, throwing long, dark shadows around us. After dark, we followed a rocky river bank, our shoes getting soaked, and set up camp under a protective stand of pines, our bed a soft blanket of pine needles. We each ate one orange for dinner before huddling up close together for warmth. Cold, wet, and miserable, we listened to the sound of the icy mountain stream gurgling past as we drifted off into a restless sleep.

We awoke at six and ate another orange each, before setting out, shaking from the cold. The river had risen several feet during the night, and its spray had drifted over us, covering us with ice crystals. My sore feet were much worse, and each step sent needles of pain through them. We climbed the steep foothills at the base of the Alps for hours. Finally we began our ascent of the mountains themselves. Each time we reached a steep summit, we expected to see the welcoming fields of Italy spread out below us. Instead, we were met with the vision of yet another, taller, peak we had yet to climb. We drank from the plentiful mountain streams, but all we had left to eat were the rinds of the oranges.

We climbed for two days. Finally, we crested a summit and looked down on a large city. What was it? We then realized it was Bellinzona. We'd gone in a giant circle. After evaluating, we set out again, heading south with new resolve not to deviate, but we were out of food and our stomachs were gnawing on themselves from hunger. A few mornings later, after a breakfast of cold water that made my stomach contract against my ribs in pain, I noticed a group of leafy green shrubs with berries on them. I called the others over and showed them. Both advised me not to eat them; it was a long way to a stomach pump or a doctor. I was fairly convinced that these were unripe blueberries from my years growing up on the farm, and I allowed my hunger to overcome my better judgment, devouring them in handfuls. Within minutes, I became dizzy and lost my sense of direction. I fell to the ground, my stomach erupting from within as if I'd swallowed sticks of dynamite. Seconds later, I began to vomit uncontrollably. We discussed what to do, and my companions agreed we had better head back to Bellinzona and give ourselves up. The Brit said he'd seen many of his friends die of food poisoning in the POW camps. I refused. At first my partners refused to leave me alone, but I finally convinced them that I would be well enough to make my way back and surrender, urged them to go on without me, and they did so with some reluctance. If they were captured, they would alert the authorities to my location so someone could come get me. Subsisting on grass and snow, I staggered back to Bellinzona, finally dropping down on one of the long wooden benches in the train station to wait for the morning train. The trip home was uneventful. In the entire 500-mile journey, I was never once questioned or asked for identification. I rode the bus up to Adelboden, made my way to my room, took a bath, and fell into bed. How many days I'd been gone, I really never knew. I'd lost all track of time.

Before sunup the next morning, I was rudely awakened by two guards who burst into my room uninvited and demanded that I follow them to the commander's office. I was roughly ushered into an office and stood before the Swiss commander. "You have broken all of Switzerland's

6. THE FIRST ESCAPE • 47

neutrality rules," he informed me. "I need a complete statement from you of your whereabouts for the past several weeks." When I filled him in, minus any information that would betray my fellow escapees, I could tell he was furious. He refused to believe that in all the time of the escape, not one Swiss guard had questioned me. I showed him my cancelled railroad stubs, which only made him angrier. How could this young, rebellious American, who looked like a skeleton, have crossed the country and made fools of the Swiss military? He was joined by another Swiss officer, who also railed at me. Once again I was struck by the fact that nearly every Swiss officer resembled the stereotypical German SS officer: tall, blond-haired and blue-eyed, cocky, and with a deep hatred of Americans. As I walked out of interrogation, an American officer joined me and told me not to worry; he would see to it that my punishment was no worse than a few weeks of confinement to my room. He also assured me that he would find a doctor to look at my feet.

Late one afternoon a few days later, as I lay on my bunk after soaking my feet, two armed Swiss soldiers walked into the room and took me out under guard. Again, I stood before the commander, who was very upset. "No one escapes from Switzerland!" he told me emphatically. "Don't you realize we have one of the best-guarded borders of any country in the world? You are very stupid."

They put me in a small, locked, closet-like room, and held me there until nightfall. After dark, two Swiss guards escorted me to a parked vehicle in the back of the building. I asked to see an American, and was told that the Americans did not know I was leaving, and that I would never see them again. The car was similar to a German two-seated command car, with side curtains in the back. One soldier was driving, and one sat on either side of me in the back seat. Feeling like a hardened criminal, I was driven to the Frutigen jail and locked into another small cell. Before they left, one of the guards informed me I was going to serve 10 days in solitary. Ten days turned into 12, and then I was released back to my old room at Adelboden.

My freedom, or a semblance of it, was short-lived, for barely a day went by before I was once again arrested and taken to the commander. This time, he was even more angry, and he raved at me while waving a book of Swiss Army regulations over his head. My punishment for escaping was not over; I was being sent to another prison, this time on orders of the Swiss High Command. This was a federal prison, and my crime was traveling in Switzerland without permission. I asked to see an American officer, or my roommate, but he informed me that under Swiss law, as a Swiss federal prisoner, I had no rights, and that no one was allowed to know where I was going. Instead, I was loaded onto the train with my guards.

Around daybreak we arrived at a small station where we were met by three soldiers accompanied by two leashed, vicious-looking German police dogs. My old guards gave the new ones an envelope, and the transfer was complete.

As we walked through town, one of my new guards asked, "What did you do to get sentenced to Wauwilermoos? Did you kill someone during the escape attempt?"

"No," I answered.

"Rape? Murder? Robbery? Espionage?"

"No," I said again. "I attempted to escape to Italy and return to my outfit."

The guard shook his head. "In that case, I can't understand why you've been sent here."

"That makes two of us," I assured him. My next stop would be hell itself.

CHAPTER 7

Entering the Gates of Hell

We walked from the village of Wauwil, located in a flat, open field in a valley surrounded by towering mountains. The foothills were covered with lush green grass upon which fat Swiss cattle grazed, and some sections near buildings had been planted with crops. The path to the prison was a simple dirt track; no cars or trucks made the journey to the prison, only the horse-drawn wagons that occasionally brought supplies or removed bodies. The prison was in the center of a large field with no trees or shrubs; escape would be difficult.

About a hundred feet from the gated entrance a large, 6-foot-high wooden stake stuck out of the ground.

"What's the stake for?" I asked the guard.

"It's for prisoners who disobey the rules," he said. "They are tied to the post, and they stand outside all night. If they are lucky enough to survive the wolves that come down out of the forest at night, they won't be unruly again."

Wauwilermoos Federal Prison sat in the middle of the meadow, a series of one-story wooden barracks surrounded by several tall barbed-wire fences. Its wooden front gate swung outward from either side on hinges. A guard house sat to one side, and inside more guards circled the perimeter, each with a fierce attack dog.

Inside the gate was a street lined with many individual wooden barracks, each surrounded by its own barbed-wire fence and gate—in effect a small prison inside a larger one. I'd held out some hope that the prison might house resistance fighters, who would be my allies. I would be honored to serve time with them. The stares I received as I passed each barrack sent a chill up and down my spine and disabused me of this notion, and I regretted not allowing myself to die in peace on the mountain.

As we approached the camp commandant's office, the guard left me with these final words: "I am sorry to bring you to this hellhole. Watch your every step. There are some awful men in here, and you are so young."

The commandant looked like a caricature of a pompous French Foreign Legion officer. He was thick-bodied and bullet-headed, and wore cavalry-style high leather boots, riding britches, and carried a horse whip. His name was André Béguin, and he was, unbeknownst to me at the time, a diehard Swiss Nazi. The guard who brought me in stood to attention and handed Béguin a large envelope that contained my records, which the corpulent figure read as he paced back in forth in front of me, occasionally pausing to look me up and down disapprovingly. Once he saw I was a soldier, he made me stand at attention. With every step he took, he smacked his boot with his riding crop, resulting in a loud cracking noise that made me jump. As he read, he would come to a section that he found particularly displeasing, and would hit his boot with his riding crop with extra force and exertion. When he opened his mouth, he had a loud, shrill, high-pitched voice. He began a five-minute harangue in German, which the guard was supposed to translate. When he did, the guard told me that I was now an enemy of the Swiss government. I had refused to obey the orders of the American attaché, Barnwell Rhett Legge, and his Swiss counterpart at our initial briefing. I recalled that at that meeting, when Legge, also decked out as a World War I cavalry officer, had warned us against escape, somebody in the back of the room had piped up and said, "What war orders are you reading?" Everybody laughed. That had made Legge angry, and he warned, "Disobey a Swiss order, and you'll pay dearly."

After Béguin had finished, I told him, through the interpreter, "I take my orders only from the American Army Air Force, and those orders are: 'When an airman falls into the hands of unfriendly forces, it is his duty to try and rejoin his own command.'"

"I was unaware that Switzerland was an unfriendly force," replied Béguin, his eyebrows arching.

"We are held under armed guard in one area," I replied, "unable to travel as we please, or leave to rejoin our own forces. If the Swiss are so friendly, what am I doing here? Also, I've been told on numerous occasions that the German Luftwaffe, and other high-ranking German military officers, can come and go across the Swiss/German border at will. If the Swiss are really so friendly toward the Americans, why can't we rejoin our forces?"

We got nowhere, obviously, and soon I was being led down the narrow dirt street between the barracks to a room that served as a warehouse, where they ordered me to remove my two-piece suit, white shirt and tie, shoes and socks, even my underwear, and issued me with an ill-fitting, horrible, wrinkled dark blue suit, shirt, socks, and a Swiss Army blanket. My shoes were like boxes, with binder-twine for laces, and were coming apart from the soles, which were full of holes. Everything itched, from the socks to the suit, and all were filthy. The waste from the person who'd worn them before me caked the pants. The wool next to my skin felt like barbed wire. I tried again to reach for my underwear, and was struck in the hand with a rifle butt.

A path led between the barracks, and again I walked a gauntlet of evil stares. Most prisoners appeared to be in their thirties or older, had grubby complexions, greasy hair, and unkempt beards. I felt like a child, all alone, surrounded by horrible creatures, even more alone because nobody else spoke English. My only protection was my blanket, and I wrapped myself tightly in it.

Barrack Nine. The very name is evil incarnate and capable of reawakening memories that no man should have to face, ever. The enclosure door was unlocked, squealed open on its hinges, and the guard pushed me inside. The building was about 10 by 30 feet, and next to the outside wall, running the full 30-foot length, was a ditch—the barrack toilet. There was a door at one end of the barrack, facing the main gate, and the ditch at the door end ran underneath the wall of the barrack and was thus used by the men on the inside as well. I found out later that we were allowed to clean our filth out of the ditch once a week, with a single pail of water. The waste would be loaded into a wheelbarrow and taken out into the fields, to be used as fertilizer.

The door swung shut behind me, slamming with a deathlike finality. Slowly my eyes adjusted to the room's dusty darkness. The floor was covered with straw, and the ditch had straw and human waste in it. Both the floor and the ditch were made of concrete. The walls were wood, unfinished on the inside, with the studs and rafters showing. There was a single blanket, doubled up, serving as a curtain on the window, and no stove.

The stench was overpowering and almost made me vomit. There was only one space left in the room, as far from the door and window as possible, so I took it. The rest of the day I paced in the small compound outside Barrack Nine, like a caged animal. While pacing, I noticed a small room behind the camp kitchen. It had no windows, though the door had a small open window covered with steel bars. This building would be a Godsend down the road.

As I walked the exterior compound, I noticed that the rest of the inmates at the prison made a point to avoid the men from my barrack. When it was time to get locked in for the night, and after my eyes adjusted to the rank darkness, I saw gaunt, demented, and cruel eyes fixed upon me. I made my way to my small area of straw, all the while being kicked and reviled by my barrack mates, and occasionally being pushed into the waste trough. I lay down and prayed, tried to become invisible, tried to sleep so that I could escape this evil place, if only temporarily.

What happened that night was beyond evil and has haunted my life ever since. I'm not sure how many men were in that barrack, but they all participated in torturing and raping me over the course of that endless night. After they were done with me, I crawled back to my corner. I needed to relieve myself, but was afraid to go past the other men. Instead, I fouled my pants where I lay.

Later, they dragged me back into the middle of the room, wedged a stick in my mouth and began shoving everything they could find into

7. ENTERING THE GATES OF HELL • 53

my mouth, making me choke. One man slapped me as hard as he could with the flats of his hands, one on each side of my head against my ears. After several crushing blows, I blacked out. When I came to, I bit down so hard on the sticks in my mouth that I broke part of my right back tooth. Finally, sated, they threw me into the trench of waste and left the barrack laughing. I crawled from the ditch and tried to wipe myself off on the straw. I noticed something was hanging out of my rectum, then realized to my horror that it was skin from inside my body. I tried to clean up with the dry spindly grass outside the barrack. I was numb. Slowly, I regained my senses and the pain hit me. I became furious. If I'd had my .50-caliber gun with me, I would have killed everyone in that camp, guilty or not, and saved plenty of rounds for the camp commander. If they had been there, I would have gladly killed every American and Swiss official who had allowed this to happen to me.

I limped to Béguin's office, ignoring the guard's motion for me to get out, and shoved open the door, yelling every cuss word a young Indiana farm kid knows. As I screamed, they looked at me like I was stark raving mad, and a nasty grin came across their faces. They listened to me rant for a while, then Béguin motioned for two of the guards to take me and throw me in the dirt. As I lay there on the ground, I realized that I was completely alone on this earth. I would never be able to escape from this evil Godforsaken place. No, I'd never leave here at all. I'd die here.

[Editor's Note: Unknown to Dan at the time, fellow crewman and escapee, Staff Sgt. Howard Melson, also ended up in Wauwilermoos. According to Melson, after he was captured on the Swiss/Italian border, he spent 30 days in solitary confinement before being sent to Wauwilermoos. "It was horrible," he writes. "I was the first American there at the time and the only one speaking English. Most of the internees were Polish, about 40 altogether. We did not have beds, and all had to sleep on the floor on 4 inches of hay and no pillows. We did have one blanket. There was no heat, hot water, soap, towels or toilet paper. We all had boils and lice to contend with."

Breakfast was black coffee and a biscuit, and the second, and final, meal of the day was soup with a thin layer of potato residue floating in the bottom. Several times, instead of soup they received a bowl of hot water with grass in it. One night, during a downpour, Melson sneaked under the fence and escaped, but was caught and forced to stand at attention for a day and a night. Eventually, Melson was transferred to another prison, but on the train, he faked being sick to his stomach, and when his captors let him go to the lavatory by himself, he managed to slip off the train, disappearing into the countryside and walking to Lyon, where he met up with the French underground.]

CHAPTER 8

The Depths of Despair

Now began the interminable period of near-nonexistence, a level of despair that was almost beyond endurance. Nights were living hell. Each night, after the worst was over and the creatures had fallen asleep, I wrapped myself in my blanket, sneaked out of the barrack, and slept on the ground between the barrack and the barbed wire. I don't remember how long I was able to do this, but I was eventually discovered by a guard and taken to Béguin, who warned me to stay inside Barrack Nine at night. If I did not, he warned, one of the guards might mistake me for an escapee and shoot me. Knowing that the guard with us spoke some English, I proceeded to try to tell Béguin the reason that I slept outside. The guard refused to translate. That night, the door to the barrack was locked, and I was trapped with the monsters inside again.

The torment continued without letup. Desperate, I finally discovered that I could crawl out of the barrack by getting into the waste ditch and swimming in it under the wall to the outside. The other men in Barrack Nine complained that I was escaping, and I was punished by being denied food for one day for disobeying orders. Rape and torture were acceptable, but not trying to survive.

As could be expected, my physical condition deteriorated rapidly. A constant stream of blood issued from my torn rectum and there was blood in my urine. When I coughed, my exhalations were laced with spatters of bright-red blood. It became hard to breathe, and my lungs felt like they were on fire all the time. I had open sores all over my body, and my buttocks was so raw I could not sit down. Nausea plagued me day and night, my vomit was filled with a yellow substance and tainted with blood.

Food was given out once a day, normally a piece of hard black bread and some type of drink, usually very weak coffee or hot water, occasionally watered-down milk. Sometimes we got a metal bowl filled with something resembling potato soup, and on Sunday, if one looked closely, one could occasionally catch sight of a piece of meat roughly the size of a pea.

I was losing my faith in God, always an integral part of my life. When I prayed at all, which wasn't often, it was for death. I didn't see how I could ever face people outside this compound again or be a functioning human being again. I didn't consider any of the people around me to be human, and would have gladly killed all of them without remorse. My love and faith in mankind was disappearing, replaced with a simmering hatred.

I would die soon. I knew it. I was little more than a scarecrow by this time, racked with disease, covered with boils, more animal than human. I forced my way into Béguin's office and unloaded the worst profanity-laced diatribe I could concoct, voicing my contempt for him, for Switzerland, for the camp, and calling him every bad name I could think of. As a coup de grâce, I added one more that I'd never used before.

"You fucking Swiss!"

The reaction was instant. Béguin knew the word, but to make sure, turned to a guard. "Voss ist this focking?" The guard hesitated, but Béguin persisted. When told, he flew into a towering rage, and ordered me thrown into the tiny building by the kitchen, the one I'd noticed upon arriving at the camp. I was sentenced to stay there for five days. This was excellent! For the first time, I would be free of my tormentors. What the commandant thought of as a harsh punishment would instead be my salvation! From then on, I tried to get in trouble, to get sentenced to that small room, and I always put on an excellent act when I was sent there, begging for mercy, resisting until the guard shoved me through the door. Once inside my haven, I prayed that they never found out the truth.

8. THE DEPTHS OF DESPAIR • 57

When I returned to Barrack Nine some time later, I noticed that all the nasty, brutish creatures who had lived there were gone, replaced with much younger men, most in their early thirties. These men were not cruel or malicious; in fact, I think they were afraid of me. When I motioned that I wanted to sleep by the door, there were no objections. The new prisoners were mostly Polish, Austrian, and Hungarian. None of them spoke English, but we got along fairly well using sign language. Every so often, one of these men actually did some small kindness. I could now sleep and heal. I spent a lot of time sleeping in the barrack now that I didn't have to fear it. The other prisoners also indicated to me that there were now some British prisoners in the camp. British prisoners! Someone to speak English with after all this time! I was thrilled but never encountered any. I asked the guards if it were true, and they concurred. But when I went to Béguin and asked to be housed with men who spoke English, he refused. He was still very angry with me for my "focking Swiss" comments.

And then, one day, salvation! Salvation in an unlikely form, but salvation nonetheless. Just as I was leaving the barrack, I saw a real live "spit and polish" British sergeant major striding confidently up the path to the camp, accompanied by a Swiss officer. I started toward him, then realized that I must look frightening and smell terrible, and held back. They started to walk around me, trying to ignore this barely human creature before them, when I spoke.

"I'm an American airman," I managed to croak, stopping the man in his tracks. His eyebrows arched upwards and he appeared stunned.

The Brit turned to the Swiss officer. "How in the world did an American soldier get in here?"

The Swiss officer shrugged his shoulders. In the 10 seconds it took for the two of them to walk the rest of the way to Béguin's office, I unloaded as much of my story as I could blurt out. Both of them tried to ignore me—the Swiss out of embarrassment that his nation could treat another human being this way, and the Brit because he didn't want to admit that any person who claimed to be part of the Allied forces would be neglected like I was in a so-called "neutral" country without the Allies knowing about it. When they arrived at the door, the two officers were admitted, but I was pushed harshly and fell down the steps onto the dirt. The Brit turned back and looked down at me, and this time I could see pity in his eyes.

"I will come see you before I leave," he said, before disappearing into the office.

How they were able to get him out of the camp without me seeing him is a mystery, but I did not see him again the rest of the day, and realized he'd left without his promised visit. This was a harsh blow to my frail body and spirit. As time passed, I realized that I was indeed alone again. Days were spent cleaning my boils and my wounds with the dew-soaked grass. I also began collecting fine sand around the barracks, and using it to brush my teeth and to scrape the layers of dirt and oil off my body. To keep myself clean, I would wash my clothes at the outside faucet several times a day, with me inside of them, and walk around wet the rest of the day. This soothed my sores. I also tucked fresh, cool grass into my shoes to soothe my frostbitten, infected, and dying feet.

Days passed, how many I do not know. But one day, the British sergeant major again strode up the path to the prison, only this time he was alone. He stopped and spoke to me. He said he was there to check up on some British prisoners in another part of the camp. I asked if he would request that I be housed with the British prisoners. He agreed to try.

"But I have my doubts," he said. "The commandant has very little love for the British, but even less for the Americans, and as I could tell from my last visit, he has only hatred for you. Besides, the British prisoners are in another part of the camp. You are housed in the high-security area, where only the most dangerous prisoners are kept. Whatever did you do to get stuck in here?"

"I tried to escape," I told him.

"That's all? I can't believe it."

I assured him it was true. He then walked into the commandant's office. I waited outside for a few minutes, then barged my way in. The commandant, not wanting to look bad in front of the Brit, let me stay. I was also permitted to talk to the sergeant, and I told him the whole sordid tale, from beginning to end, leaving out nothing. The guard

8. THE DEPTHS OF DESPAIR • 59

who spoke some English occasionally translated some of what I said for Béguin, and he began to look nervous and angry.

"I'm in very bad health," I told the British sergeant major. "I have boils and sores all over my body. My feet were frostbitten on a mission and have been infected ever since. I have a hard time even catching a breath, and when I cough, I cough up blood. But even so, I've never once been allowed to see a doctor, not at any time. Why was I put into Barrack Nine, and subjected to all that horrible abuse? Why wasn't the American air attaché informed I was here? Why aren't they trying to find out where one of their American airmen has disappeared to? Why doesn't the Red Cross come to the prison and inspect it?"

The sergeant, speaking very good German, was relaying my comments and complaints to Béguin, and they were soon embroiled in a heated argument. After they calmed down a bit, I was asked to unbutton my coat, roll up my pant legs, and remove my shoes so that they could see my sores, boils, and infections. And before they could stop me, I pulled down my pants and showed them the skin protruding from my rectum, and the burning red infected skin around my anus and buttocks.

The guard almost immediately grabbed my pants and pulled them back up, but it was apparent that they had seen more than they bargained for. Now, due to the exertion and excitement, I began to cough, and blood spewed from my mouth into my hands. As I coughed, the men in the room edged away from me. The commandant told the sergeant that he thought I had tuberculosis and other diseases that might be contagious. The sergeant continued to answer questions for me, but now did so from a safe distance.

"The commandant here says this is a federal prison, not a POW camp," the sergeant major told me. "The Red Cross has no authority over federal prisons. The American attaché and the brigadier general in charge of internees are not concerned about you. You have disobeyed orders by attempting to escape. As far as they are concerned, you are no longer an American soldier. As to the doctor visit, the commandant here says it's too expensive to bring in a doctor to see just one prisoner."

He then took me aside and explained, "You are in the worst camp in Switzerland. The commandant has little feeling for any other human beings, but especially Americans, because not too long ago, Americans bombed a Swiss city by mistake. Also, the Swiss in this part of the country are pro-German. This camp, Wauwilermoos, is much, much worse than the Italian or German POW camps I've been in. Those are run by ex-combat military officers who have more compassion for soldiers than this Swiss commandant, who's never fought in a war, but only wears the uniform for prestige."

When the sergeant major returned days later, he bore bad news. His superior officer had talked to Legge personally, and Legge had told him that "this soldier broke Swiss law, so he is in the hands of the Swiss government." He then took me directly to Béguin's office, on the way again informing me that Wauwilermoos was the worst prison in Switzerland and Béguin one of the most sadistic tyrants in the Swiss prison system. He asked if I'd been given any medical treatment since his last visit, to which the answer was no. He then told Béguin in no uncertain terms that he, the British sergeant major, was taking my case to the highest levels of the American and British embassies in Bern.

He'd told me, but didn't tell Béguin, that the Americans had refused to admit that I was even at Wauwilermoos, but that if I were, I'd probably be getting out soon.

As he prepared to leave, I told him, in desperation, that I'd never had a trial at any point. It was true. I hadn't. I'd been sentenced without benefit of a trial. Armed with this information, the Brit rushed back in and confronted Béguin, and when he came out he was smiling. There was one thing that the Swiss had great respect for, and that was the law.

"Those dirty bastards, putting you through this hell, and never even giving you a trial!" he said, and promised me that all hell was going to break loose over this, and he walked out of the camp with a jaunty step. I watched him disappear down the road toward the village, and for the first time, I let myself wonder if maybe this man, now no more than a speck in the distance, really would be able to get me out.

A few days later, I was ordered to Béguin's office. It was cold and I shivered as I entered, and to my surprise, I was allowed to walk up and warm myself at the pot belly stove that blazed in the office. I'd been cold for so long that I'd forgotten what it felt like to be warm. I

8. THE DEPTHS OF DESPAIR • 61

soaked up the warmth from the stove, and would have crawled inside if I could have.

There were three men in the office, with two of the largest, meanest-looking German police dogs I'd ever seen. "We're taking you to Baden for trial," I was told. Dressed in my ratty suit and my boxy shoes, I strode out of the camp, to the silent waving salutes of many of my fellow prisoners—showing their support in the only way they knew how. At the train station in Wauwil, the other passengers gave me a wide berth, their eyes as big as saucers. Who was this dangerous, hardened criminal in their midst? There, and on the train, people stared at me like a freak in a cage. I wanted to scream at them, "My God, people, all I did was try to escape from your country and return to mine!" but I didn't know their language, and they would not have believed me in any case.

In Baden, we went to a law office. The guards and dogs stayed. A well-dressed man walked in, looked me up and down, and informed me in good English that he would be representing me at my trial. When we entered the courtroom, I noted that the guards in the hallway came to rigid attention and shot snappy salutes at my so-called lawyer. That son-of-a-bitch lawyer was nothing more than a high-ranking Swiss officer. I said this out loud so that he could hear me. "I've already been found guilty. This trial is for looks only." If looks could kill, I would have been dead when he turned his head back toward me. In the courtroom were my two fellow escapees, the ball turret gunner and the Brit. We were all on trial at the same time.

There were six judges, and the evidence was presented. The trial was conducted in German. When it was over, I asked my defender what my sentence was. He refused to answer me. I screamed out in the courtroom, so that everyone could hear, "You mean you're sending me back to that hellhole, Wauwilermoos?" The defender finally answered yes. As I left, I was given a transcript of the trial in English. It made no reference to how long I would have to stay at Wauwilermoos. Perhaps I would be there forever. And as to my ball turret gunner or the British soldier, I never saw them in Switzerland again.

I returned to Barrack Nine and an unknown future. A few days later, the British sergeant major visited to see some British prisoners.

62 • PRISONER OF THE SWISS

He told me he was working on my case, but that it was hard because the Americans were not cooperating. Every time I spoke with him, my bitterness against the American government worsened, especially toward Legge. He'd spent many years in the position as attaché, even riding out the war there. When American airmen began landing in Switzerland, it made his glamorous, party-filled life more complicated. If we hadn't appeared, he could have ridden out the war enjoying cocktail parties, impressing everyone with his polished cavalry uniform with medals hanging all over his chest. When the Brit returned from checking on his men, he asked if anyone from the American side had come to check on me yet. I answered in the negative.

"That's very strange," he said. "As I understand it, the attaché has assigned several American officers who are also interned to travel all over Switzerland and keep track of all the interned enlisted men, and of their treatment." He mused that maybe they were too busy chasing the Swiss women, or, worse yet, that the Americans were not even aware of Wauwilermoos' existence. Again I had a coughing fit, and he went to complain to Béguin.

"If this American dies in here because he receives no medical treatment," he told Béguin, "he and the British government will personally have the Swiss government and the camp commandant charged with his death."

Béguin eyed him with curiosity. "Why should you or the British care about this American, if his own government doesn't?"

"Because he is a human being, and one of our allies who fought against Hitler!" He told me that Béguin the diehard Nazi looked none too pleased with the anti-Hitler comment. He also warned me that Béguin would not be above using treachery to get me killed or sentenced to a life term and to be on my guard at all times.

The first strange occurrence happened only a few days later, when an immaculately uniformed American enlisted man sauntered into the camp. I figured he was probably a Swiss undercover agent, especially after he was put in Barrack Nine, though we were full up and other barracks were not. He moved in and slept right next to me that night. Apparently, he was a B-17 crewman who had been shot down and sent to Wauwilermoos. He was from Kansas City, Missouri. We talked a lot

8. THE DEPTHS OF DESPAIR • 63

and the next day he made several trips to Béguin's office. The second night I woke to find myself back in solitary. I don't remember how I got there; I must have been so sick with TB by then that I passed out and they'd moved me to isolate me from the other prisoners.

During my second day in the hole, they came and got me and brought me before Béguin. What were they going to charge me with now, I wondered?

A guard translated. "The commandant, out of the goodness of his heart, wants you to visit a restaurant in Nebikon. Some good Swiss restaurant food may help bring back your health and be good for the boils all over your body."

Flabbergasted, I responded that I had no money. Béguin reached into his pocket and handed me the Swiss equivalent of a five-dollar bill. I instinctively thanked him, and as the guard escorted me through the gate he warned me, "Any attempt to escape will bring the worst punishment—even death."

As I left, the mysterious American waved cheerily at me and called out, "Good luck and good eating!" Later, I wondered how he could have known where I was going, or that I was eating.

I walked unsteadily down the narrow wagon track toward the town of Nebikon, near Wauwil. The pass was good for four hours, but with my weak body and bad feet, I wasn't sure I could make it to town, let alone there and back, in the allotted time.

As I walked, I was plagued with the uneasy feeling that I was being followed and watched. Just as I entered the village, a soft voice called out to me. Standing next to a large tree was the most beautiful girl I had ever seen, more beautiful than my imagination could have concocted. I looked at her and then at myself—a filthy, boil-covered skeleton clothed in rags, and wondered if she was really speaking to me. She had dark, wavy auburn hair that glistened in the sun as it spilled down her back. This was no Swiss mountain farm girl, that much was plain. She motioned me to the tree, reached out both her hands, and took my dirty ones in hers.

"Are you the American from Wauwilermoos?" I said yes, and we sat down on the grass. When she sat down, she pulled her dress up slightly above her knees, revealing her shapely legs. I had not really looked at a girl in a long time.

We began talking.

"I'm Austrian, and my mother and I escaped here because of the war," she told me. "We fled after the Nazis imprisoned my father for refusing to join the German Army. After arriving in Switzerland and making our way to Zurich, we were reported to the Swiss Secret Police for not having Swiss identification when we applied to work at a restaurant. The Swiss Secret Police threatened to deport us, but gave us the option of working for the Swiss Nazi Party, and we chose the lesser of two evils."

"What kind of services do you provide for the Swiss Nazi Party?" I asked her.

"Anything we are asked to do."

Belatedly, a loud bell began to go off in my head. I remembered the British sergeant major's warning against treachery, and a tall Hungarian I'd seen at Wauwilermoos who had been sentenced to life in prison for having a relationship with an underage Swiss girl.

"Are you trying to trap me?" I asked. "Are you working with the commander of Wauwilermoos?"

"Yes," she said.

"Are you the girl used to trap the Hungarian?" Again she assented.

"I am also the commander's girl," she said.

"How old are you?"

"I'm 15."

"And you are his mistress, and work for the Swiss Secret Police?"

"Yes."

She asked what my crime was, that they were trying so hard to entrap me with an underage girl. I told her that I was in prison for attempting to escape from Switzerland.

"I'll tell them you refused my advances," she said. "Men often do, fearing a trap. Or I can tell them you were too dirty and I was worried of catching a disease from you." She assured me that she would not be in trouble for failing in her mission.

From then on, we stayed in highly visible places, and walked through the village. The villagers refused to say hello to her, and looked at me with distaste. Either the villagers did not know her at all, or they knew her as an unsavory outsider. At the end of the visit, she waved goodbye and I returned to the prison. I was thrown back into solitary. I reached the end of my rope, and the last thing I remember is trying to kill myself, stuffing straw down my throat, raving like a madman. And then there were fingers prying open my mouth, pulling out the straw, pushing on my stomach. I dimly saw the burly figure of the British sergeant major above me, and then I vomited and everything went black.

CHAPTER 9

Hospital

This part of my story is the hardest to write, for it is a time filled with blackouts, a period where time has no meaning. I am writing it as I experienced it, and if the reader is occasionally confused, then he or she is in the same condition I was in as I lived it.

Even to this day, I have no idea how I got to the hospital in Lucerne, or what happened after I got there. I only know that when I woke up, I thought I had died and was in heaven. I was in an all-white room, lying in a bed. A large cross hung on the wall at the foot of the bed. When I tried to move, I began floating away, and my mind went blank. This happened several times. I remember waking up, staring at the cross on the wall, and wondering if I was dead or alive. Finally, I stayed awake long enough to take brief inventory of my surroundings.

Something was stuck into my arm, and a tube ran from it to a glass bottle on a stand fastened to the headboard. An oxygen mask covered my nose and mouth, and my whole body was slathered in ointment or salve and then covered with a thin cloth similar to cheesecloth.

My bowels seemed about to explode, and I tried to get up, only to find my wrists and ankles tied to the bed. A male orderly dressed in white came in and administered a shot, and I drifted away. Every time I came to, they did this, and I soon realized that I was relieving myself in a diaper they had me wearing.

One day, I awoke to a vision, and I was certain I had died and gone to heaven. A lady, dressed in a long white dress and robe, hovered at

9. HOSPITAL • 67

the foot of my bed. A string of beads dangled out of her billowy sleeve, and she had a white bonnet on her head, completely covering her hair. She wore a large cross and a face mask. The beads clicked together as she moved them with her fingers. I started coughing, spitting up blood, and I knew I was not in heaven, because our Sunday school teachers back home always told us that there is no sickness in heaven. The lady in white took off my oxygen mask and placed a basin under my face to catch the blood as I coughed.

I awoke to find myself no longer tied into bed. Nothing was attached to my arm, nor was my body smeared with ointment or gauze. Each boil on my body had been covered separately with gauze and tape; I had dozens of them on my face and body. My head was shaved, and the boils on my head were anointed and bandaged. I realized I was in a Catholic hospital, and the woman in white was a nun. There were other nuns who came in from time to time to treat me, but none of them spoke. On one side of me a strange fellow lay and stared at me all day and all night; when I turned my back, I could feel his eyes burning into my back. On the other side of me was an Indian wearing a turban who had the longest handlebar mustache I'd ever seen. His chart said he was a British soldier, but he looked more like a skeleton covered in brown wrapping paper. All three of us had occasional bad coughing spells, after which we were treated with a red liquid that had a minty taste.

It had been five months since my feet had frozen—five months with no treatment—but now, in the hospital, each time the bandages were removed from them, there was real and noticeable improvement. Also, I was eating, building my strength. At first, I couldn't hold any food down; eventually, I could stomach some soup, black bread, and particularly bananas. I hadn't had any fruit in a long time, and I ate as many as I could stand.

I watched the Indian. No one could be skinnier and still be alive. He sat on his bed for hours on end, playing with his long, curling moustache with his legs crossed under him. Occasionally he would slither off the bed and crawl over to the open window to soak up the sun, again sitting on his legs. He always seemed to be in some kind of trance. The more I watched him move, the more I thought he looked like a snake. He

68 • PRISONER OF THE SWISS

didn't move, he slithered. As my condition improved, my imagination began to run amok, and I was highly bothered by the fact that the Indian actually was a snake.

Weeks passed. One day a man came in wearing a white sack over his head, with holes cut for the eyes. It was the sergeant major. He looked ridiculous and I told him so, and for the first time in many months, I actually laughed out loud, and so did he. The laughter was contagious and pretty soon the entire room was laughing. The sergeant shook my hand, then went over to the Indian soldier and talked with him in English. He then came back and told me that they'd had to move me from Wauwilermoos by stretcher to the train station, then in a heated mail car to Lucerne. In Lucerne, they had operated on my rectum, which had been badly torn by the bastards in Barrack Nine.

The doctor told the sergeant that there was nothing they could do for my ears; my eardrums were scarred from the beatings, but he thought over time they might heal themselves. He had also removed my broken back tooth. The doctor said that he'd never seen a man closer to death, but that I was healing fast now, and would soon be sent to a tuberculosis sanitarium in Davos. The sergeant major told me he couldn't stay long. I took his hands, looked him in the eyes, and thanked him for saving my life. His only reply was that he now had a very different view of the American military, seeing as how they had neglected one of their warriors when he needed help so badly. He then departed through a swinging door.

I never saw or heard from him again. But I will never forget him.

I was transferred to a large tuberculosis sanitarium in Davos. There were other patients who were very sick and needed to be accompanied on their walks, and the staff asked if I would like to help. I especially enjoyed walking two very pretty, very sick girls. These two looked like walking skeletons, and we had to walk at a snail's pace, but we could make it to a bench that looked out over a lovely vista. One could literally see for miles; I was told that on a clear day, you could see all the way into Austria.

Before a walk one morning, I had a visitor, an Air Force officer from the American attaché in Bern. My pilot had managed to get them to track me down to the sanitarium. When I told him I'd been in Wauwilermoos, the officer confessed he'd never heard of it. "All I know is that you broke Swiss laws and were sent to a place forbidden to everyone except the Swiss military," he explained. "At one time, the Swiss told us that you were killed trying to escape. I'll be giving you some instructions soon, but if you think you're in danger of being captured, you need to destroy them immediately. Your pilot has been told that you are in great danger. Do not trust anybody. He's paying the Swiss underground a lot of money to arrange your escape. You'll get a forged passport, then travel to Geneva. There, you'll get help crossing the border into France, and will pass into the hands of the French underground. Your crew will meet you at the border and you will all cross together."

The new plan made me worry. With all that I'd gone through, I didn't know if I had another escape in me, but I didn't want to let my pilot down, and I agreed to try.

One thing was certain—I would rather die than be taken back to Wauwilermoos.

CHAPTER 10

The Second Escape

I clutched two passes and railroad tickets in my sweating hands, tickets that would get me from Davos to Bern and from Bern to Geneva. One pass showed my photograph and used my real name; the other was in the name of an American captain, issued by the American attaché in Bern, allowing the captain to travel anywhere in Switzerland.

This escape had been a scary and tough decision. I was still quite sick and weak from my ordeals. Just walking up the hill to the bench where I liked to sit left me gasping for breath. Would my body hold up during the escape? I had also grown to love working at the TB hospital in Davos, helping the other patients.

After all I'd been through, could I still travel without arousing suspicion? What if I were stopped? Would I panic, gripped with the fear of being sent back to Wauwilermoos? I finally made up my mind. Despite my weakened condition and fragile mental health, I was not going to let my pilot down. I was barely 20, and felt an intense loyalty to my country and my pilot. The final walk with the two dying girls was emotionally devastating. They had seen my visitor, and though not a word had been said, they sensed I would be leaving them, and they held my arm extra tightly that day.

Now here I was, standing at the Davos train station, waiting for the train that would begin my journey to freedom. Davos and Geneva are about as far apart as two places can be in Switzerland, one on each end of the country, east and west. In Bern, I was supposed to change trains

10. THE SECOND ESCAPE • 71

and catch a second to Geneva. Once in Geneva, the plan was to make my way to a particular restaurant, and take a seat. When the waiter came over, I would give him a password, he would then buy me a drink, and a second person would escort me to the back kitchen. From there, I'd be taken to a rendezvous point, meet up with my pilot, co-pilot, and bombardier, and we'd take a taxi to a place where the road ran parallel to the Swiss/French border. The French side at this point was much lower than the Swiss side, and was protected by three massive rolls of barbed wire, each about 5 feet across and stacked in a pyramid 10 feet high. We'd jump out of the car, run to the wire, scale it, and dash to freedom.

I had tried to dress like a typical Swiss traveler. I wore a baggy blue suit with short legs, and high-topped, thick-soled shoes, both of which were the common dress of a Swiss laboring man. The only thing missing was a hat. I carried only my handkerchief with a few personal items wrapped in it, and a pocketbook with my papers. The most valuable paper in my possession was the paper, on Swiss government stationery and signed by the six judges, from my trial in Baden with the word "Wauwilermoos" written on it; with this, I had proof of the prison's existence. The Swiss would try to deny it, and the Americans would believe them, but with this paper, I felt I had a chance.

The first leg of the journey went smoothly. As we passed through a small station somewhere past Bern, I was surprised to see my bombardier standing on the platform. I motioned discreetly to him, and he boarded and sat down with me. Shortly after Lausanne, our train followed the edge of a giant lake, and I heard someone say it was Lake Geneva. We traveled its shore for miles, drawing ever closer to the city itself. As we approached Geneva, I looked around and noticed that every man on the train was wearing a hat. Nervously, I looked at my bombardier. No, he wasn't wearing a hat either. A major mistake. Would we be noticed and caught over something as simple as this? I began to sweat, and to take my mind off it, I tried to look out the window, but I felt like a large ugly head without a hat that was obvious to all.

Geneva was the end of the line. All passengers would debark here. As I worked my way down the crowded aisle, my heart skipped a beat. A group of soldiers was approaching our coach. I tried to walk a little faster, bumping into the people in front of me in the aisle and getting annoyed "back off" looks in return. My bombardier was slightly ahead of me. Suddenly, a tall Swiss officer reached into the passing crowd and roughly jerked my bombardier out of it, jostling other passengers aside. The blood froze in my veins. I wanted desperately to run, but restrained myself. In any case, I was jammed into the aisle with other passengers in front of and behind me, and all I could do was shuffle forward. As my foot touched the bottom step, a large hand closed around my arm and pulled me through the crowd, nearly yanking me out of my oversized shoes. I fell hard to the concrete platform. Several other passengers appeared poised to object to the rough treatment, but saw the glower from my soldier captor and thought better of it.

Soon we stood nearly alone on the platform. There were three Swiss officers and two Swiss soldiers, and they had pulled several other passengers aside as well. There was little doubt in my mind—they'd been waiting for us.

The Swiss officer who'd captured my bombardier was a cocky mean bastard, the kind I had learned to despise, and his rough treatment of my superior officer made my blood boil. "Let go of him, you dirty, fucking Swiss bastard," I yelled, and was instantly smashed in the face and fell down. The other soldiers intervened, and my bombardier reached down, helped me up, and muttered for me to take it easy, he could take care of himself if need be, but right now we were at their mercy.

The cocky officer addressed us in perfect English. "You are Americans on unauthorized leave." I pulled out the second pass, the one that had allowed the American officer to travel all over Switzerland with no restrictions, and the officer glanced at it briefly. He then turned back to my bombardier, speaking in a disrespectful tone. "You are a liar. I know you are not supposed to be in Geneva." He then turned to me: "I don't believe that you are the captain shown on this pass."

I knew the gig was up. My legs were weak and all I could think of was Wauwilermoos. There was no way I'd go back there. Should I make a run for it and let them gun me down?

Then a strange thing happened. The officer noticed the first pass, the one with my real name and information on it, and scrutinized it with

10. THE SECOND ESCAPE • 73

great care. He asked again for the other pass, and the soldiers stood in a huddle, off to one side, looking from one pass to another, speaking in German and occasionally shooting glances my way. The officer walked back over to me.

"Are you Culler?"

They had been looking for me. Maybe they'd let my bombardier and the other captured men go? The officer directed the other captured men to leave with a few of the soldiers. Before my bombardier was led away, he broke away, rushed over, and shook my hand.

"Good luck," he said, "I'll see you after the war."

I returned the wishes, but knew I'd never make it home. I was going to be sent back to Wauwilermoos. But I'd figure out a way to die first.

The officer escorted me into a building. Without any emotion, he handed me the pass with my real name on it.

"Go," he said, motioning with his thumb.

I was dumbfounded. "Where?"

"Wherever you were going before we stopped you," he said, a slight smile drawing across his thin lips.

"Well, then, where did you take my bombardier?"

"To the military police station. He'll be released to the American embassy in Geneva."

"Why couldn't he and I go together?"

"Because he is an officer, and you are not."

I couldn't get over the complete change in his demeanor. However, I also couldn't forget how violently he'd slapped me on the platform. Perhaps I was not thinking straight, but before I knew it, I had asked him for directions to the restaurant where we were supposed to meet. This may sound stupid, but remember that I was mixed up, untrained for what to do in an escape or evasion, and stressed from the journey. In any case, I couldn't shove the words back into my mouth, so there was nothing to do but move forward. In perfect English, the officer gave directions. He then held out his hand, and I shook it, the same hand that had slapped me so hard only minutes earlier.

"Have a good time. Geneva is a wonderful city and has many things to see."

74 • PRISONER OF THE SWISS

Walking away, an uneasy feeling gripped me. There was something inherently evil in his kindness.

I walked the two or three blocks to the restaurant, glancing back from time to time to make sure I wasn't being followed. The place was crowded, filled mostly with older, well-dressed men. A few women sat at tables in the middle, and the walls were lined with tall booths. I sat in the only empty booth, two booths from the front door and a long walk to the back kitchen, feeling conspicuous in my ugly suit and hillbilly shoes.

A waiter hustled by. I motioned to him, but he ignored me. The next time he passed, he glared as if he were annoyed that a tattered individual such as myself had taken up an entire booth. I kept motioning to him, and after a while, he approached the table to wait on me, speaking to me in French. I ordered a cup of coffee in English, and gave him the password. He ignored me and walked back to the kitchen, returning with a cup of coffee. I waited. Nothing happened. I motioned to the waiter again, and he came over. I ordered another cup of coffee. Instead of refilling the cup, as one would in an American restaurant, he brought me a new cup. Again I gave the password, and he ignored it and walked away. The more I was ignored, and the longer I waited, the more intense the stares from the well-dressed men in the other booths. It was ludicrous, but before long, I sat in the booth with a half-dozen cups of coffee, each of which I'd responded to with the password.

There was one booth nearby that never cleared out during that time. Four men sat at it, drinking coffee, and staring at me.

It was getting on toward mid-afternoon. I'd drunk so much coffee at this point that my teeth were floating and I doubted I'd sleep for a week. Maybe I had the wrong waiter? I ordered some more coffee from other waiters, again giving the password, again being ignored. It was doubtful by this time that I would ever sleep again.

Suddenly it hit me. Maybe I was in the wrong restaurant?

This place had a sign that said "café" instead of restaurant. Had I been in the wrong place this whole time? I had no way to check; we had all destroyed our instructions in case of capture. Finally, in desperation, I began to saunter casually back toward the kitchen. As I did so, I could literally feel four pairs of eyes burning holes in the back of my jacket. I caught my foot on a chair leg and stumbled, causing a racket. Now everybody in the entire restaurant was staring at me. This was not going well at all. I felt like I might as well just jump up and down and yell: "Look at me! I'm an American and I'm escaping!" Picking myself up, I flew into the kitchen.

I hurtled in, and said the password to the first person I saw. Quick as lightning, a meaty hand grabbed me, and suddenly I was being dragged through the kitchen, hitting everyone in my path, and out the back door into the alley behind the restaurant.

"Stupid! Stupid! Stupid!" the huge man growled at me. "Are you Culler or the bombardier?"

"Culler."

"You idiot. The place is swarming with Swiss Secret Police! They're probably looking for you! They came in shortly before you did. Somebody informed."

"Is the rest of my crew here?"

"Yes, they're hiding already. You may have jeopardized the whole mission with your antics. This place has been watched for some time. I'm not sure how long we'll be able to operate. You have given yourself away, and now I'm not sure we'll be able to get you or your people out at all."

I felt about one inch tall.

He held me in the alley for a long time. "If the police come back here looking for you, I will turn you over to them. A lot of good and powerful people will be hurt if you tell the police or military about this operation. Your life or freedom is not worth what this operation means to a lot of the people higher up, in and out of Switzerland!"

We waited for the police to come get me. Minutes passed. No one came. He finally pushed me up some steps and into an upper room over the café. There, to my relief and delight, stood my pilot and co-pilot. I hadn't seen them for many months and had gone through hell since, and tears welled up in my eyes.

"Where's the bombardier? Has he arrived yet?" I asked.

76 • PRISONER OF THE SWISS

"No," they replied.

"He came with me on the train, but we got separated at the station. I think they may have been looking for us. The commander at Wauwilermoos doesn't want me to leave Switzerland alive." Neither of them had ever heard the name Wauwilermoos, and none of the underground members had either. A man came in and told us that the bombardier was safe, but would be in military hands for a few days.

"We can't wait," he admonished.

"You said that about waiting for our engineer, too," said the pilot. Still, they had refused pressure to leave without me.

"The bombardier is another matter," said the pilot. "He's been moving freely around Switzerland for the past several months and knows his way around. He'll get out all right and we'll meet up with him again in England. Now, we have to go!"

"A taxi will be here any minute," said one of our conspirators. As if on cue, another man ran in and announced our ride was waiting. We hustled down the outside stairs and into the darkened alley, piling into the waiting taxi, all three of us wedged into the narrow back seat, and the taxi sped away like a rocket. We zipped through the streets of Geneva at breakneck speed—a speed that seemed reckless and could get us pulled over. Geneva has many curving streets, and we were thrown first one way, then the other, in the rear seat as the tires screeched around each corner.

Finally, we approached the outskirts of Geneva. The driver slowed down and stopped on the verge, holding out his hand and asking to see the money. My pilot pulled out a sheaf of Swiss paper bills, flashed them to the approving nod of the driver, and then quickly stashed them between the back seat cushion and the backrest. Before we started up again, our driver had me move to the right side of the back seat, making me the last person who would jump out when we reached the barbed wire. We then accelerated back up to bullet-like speed, the Swiss countryside zipping by our window in a blur of greens and yellows. Was I being set up? Why had the driver moved me at the last minute?

"We're getting close!" shouted the driver. We scanned the road ahead for signs of the uneven ground with the pyramid of barbed wire, but

IO. THE SECOND ESCAPE • 77

all I could see ahead was a road curving to our right. To our left lay a rectangular open field about a half-mile long and 200 yards wide. To the left of the field was a thick wood, and beyond the field a flat pasture curved in toward us. We all saw the rolls of barbed wire at the edge of the pasture at the same time.

Instead of speeding up to the point where we would jump out, our driver inexplicably began to slow down. Soon we were moving at a crawl.

"What are you doing? Speed up!" shouted the pilot, but the driver continued moving at a snail's pace, his eyes scanning the woods and the open field as if he were expecting company. In a flash, our driver jammed on the breaks, throwing us against the seat in front of us. Without looking back, he gesticulated wildly and hollered, "Out! Out! Out!!" The barbed wire was at least 200 yards ahead of us, necessitating a long sprint, a 10-foot climb, and a 10-foot traverse of the three large prickly rolls. Even a trained athlete would have had a difficult time completing this task.

"Please forgive me," I muttered to my friends. "Because of me, we're now all going to die."

We hesitated, and when we did, the driver pulled the door open and angrily hollered, "OUT!"

The pilot jumped out, followed by the co-pilot. Not trusting the driver or the sudden change of seating, I jumped out the right side and met up with them at the front of the car. As I passed the driver's window, my eyes met his for a split-second, and in that instant, I knew. The truth flashed before me. That bastard was in cahoots with the café people. It was a setup from the opening bell.

We ran as fast as our legs and the uneven ground allowed, and soon we were halfway across the open field. Suddenly, the air was filled with the sounds of gunfire. I could hear the bullets whizzing very near to us. Whoever it was, they were not firing over our heads—they were aiming to kill. We separated, and it seemed that most of the bullets were coming at me. There were so many gunshots that it was evident that there were multiple individuals shooting at us as we broke for the wire. As happens in a nightmare, the harder I ran, the farther away the stack of barbed wire seemed to get. It felt like I was running in slow motion.

I felt a puff as a bullet perforated my baggy pants, then another as one whipped through my flapping coat, but neither hit my body. Even if I'd been hit, I believe I would have kept running, fueled by adrenaline alone. Even if I'd been shot dead, my adrenaline and my momentum would have carried me to freedom.

We converged on the low spot in the wire, where the French side dipped down below the Swiss side, all three of us barreling up the pile, feeling the coils bounce and give under our weight. We fell into it, the barbs tearing into our clothes and puncturing our skin, but we kept going, leaving part of our clothing behind as we tumbled down into France.

"I'm hit!" It was our pilot, and we staggered to a safe spot a few yards from the border and assessed his wound. We rolled up his pant leg and found he'd been hit in the ankle. The bullet had entered one side and exited the other, but there was no way to know the extent of the damage. As we crouched there, we saw over a dozen Swiss soldiers trudge out of the woods next to the field. Half of them had their rifles pointed at the taxi driver, the other half at us. Several of the men approached, and we were staring down the barrels of six rifles. One of the soldiers spoke to us in French.

"Let's just get up and start walking slowly," said the pilot. "I don't think the Swiss will want to explain why three Americans were shot in the back this close to the border."

We walked slowly away, and the Swiss lowered their rifles and watched us go.

We were free.

A P-51 Mustang that crash-landed in Buchs, St Gallen, in February 1945.

A Consolidated B-24 Liberator in flight. *(U.S. Army, public domain)*

Postcard showing the resort of Adelboden before the war.

The Telford Crew during training in the United States. Dan's pilot, 1st Lt. George D. Telford, is at the top row left. Dan is third from right, kneeling. *(Dan Culler)*

The Telford Crew posing with *Hell's Kitten* at Shipdam in England, 1944. The crew consisted of 1st Lt. George D. Telford, pilot; 1st Lt. Francis Coune, co-pilot; 1st Lt. Donald H. McConell, Jr., navigator; 1st Lt. William E. Carroll, bombardier; T/Sgt. Daniel L. Culler, engineer/top turret gunner; T/Sgt. Francis J. Testa, radio operator; S/Sgt. James H. Hancock, right waist gunner; S/Sgt. George A. Petrik, left waist gunner; S/Sgt Howard E. Melson, ball turret gunner; and S/Sgt. John J. Hughes, tail turret gunner. *(Dan Culler)*

Above: B-24 Liberator bombers of the 44th Bomb Group line up for takeoff at Shipdam, England. (*44th Bomb Group*)

Left: A photo of a youthful Dan Culler. (*Dan Culler*)

Below: The Martin electric gun turret, used by Dan on the B-24 as top turret gunner. (*U.S. Army, public domain*)

A 44th Bomb Group ground crew works on an engine at Shipdam. (*44th Bomb Group*)

A rare photo of Hell's Kitten, taken at the 44th's base at Shipdam. (*44th Bomb Group*)

The Telford Liberator after landing at Dübendorf, Switzerland. (*Dani Egger, Swiss Warbirds, warbird.ch*)

General Barnwell Rhett Legge, military attaché in Switzerland during World War II. (*Army Signal Corps, public domain*)

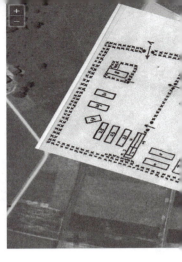

Swiss internee Bob Carroll on the street in the internee village of Davos Platz, Switzerland. The internees enjoyed a great deal of freedom—as long as they didn't try to escape. (*Dwight Mears*)

An Army aerial surveillance photo taken in 1943 shows Wauwilermoos Prison. The U.S. did not officially acknowledge the prison's existence until the 1990s. (*U.S. Army, public domain*)

An idyllic image of Adelboden from the early half of the 1900s. Dan spent the early part of his captivity here before escaping. (*Wikimedia Commons*)

Lt. George W. Mears, here shown as a flight cadet, grandfather of West Point historian Dwight Mears, was interned in Switzerland and imprisoned at Wauwilermoos. He inspired Dwight to advocate for the Prisoner of War Medal for Wauwilermoos prisoners. (*Dwight Mears*)

Two photographs of Lt. George W. Mears during his pilot training. *(Dwight Mears)*

Death was always waiting. This dramatic photo shows the 493rd Bomb Group's *Little Warrior* engulfed in flames on a June 28, 1944 mission over Germany. Only one man managed to parachute out, but he was killed on the ground by angry German citizens. (*U.S. Army, public domain*)

Commander André Béguin, a Swiss Nazi who administered the camp – and embezzled funds from it. He was responsible for the harsh conditions and torture endured by Dan Culler and others. (*Swiss Internee Website*)

This page and opposite, top: Interned planes at the Swiss airport of Dubendorf. At the end of the war, all were scrapped in Switzerland or England. *(Dani Egger)*

Dwight Mears *(U.S. Army official photograph)*

Six of the seven then-surviving members of the 1st Lt. George Telford Crew in 1988. Photo taken by Roy Thomas in September 1988 at the reunion in Dayton, Ohio. Roy believes this is the first time the men had been together since the war. One man did not attend. Front row, L-R: Daniel A. Culler, Howard E. Melson, George A. Petrick. Rear, L-R: George D. Telford, Francis L. Coune and William E. Carroll. (*Roy Thomas*)

A photo of Dan Culler, taken in 2014 by Swiss film-maker Daniel Wyss for an upcoming documentary. (*Daniel Wyss*)

Air Force Chief of Staff Gen. Mark Welsh, right, accompanied by Army Maj. Dr Dwight Mears, left, applauds retired Lt. Col. James Misuraca after presenting him with the Prisoner of War Medal, April 30, 2014 during a ceremony at the Pentagon. (*Cliff Owens, Associated Press, in* Military Times)

A contemporary satellite photograph shows that Wauwilermoos has been completely obliterated. (*Dwight Mears*)

The site of the Waulilermoos Prison today. (*Daniel Wyss*)

CHAPTER 11

Out of the Depths

Seventy years later, the questions linger in my mind. But one thing is not a question. To me, it is a cold, hard truth. The incident at the border was a carefully planned trap. Nobody will ever convince me otherwise. I don't think it was all the work of a mad Swiss commandant, but perhaps he had help from Swiss and American higher-ups who thought that the truth might be too uncomfortable in the post-war world, for whom the sacrifice of one man was a small price to pay for the soothing-over of wartime differences.

In any case, we were free, and the three of us—the wounded pilot in the center using us as his support—made our way out of the field, over a wall, and down a dirt road. The sky filled with foreboding dark clouds. "We have to get picked up before dark," said our pilot. "My contacts said that we don't want to be wandering around at night in this area. A person is likely to find his throat slashed by the French underground looking for Nazis or by Nazis trying to get back to Germany." The officers had navigational training, and they determined we should head north. After walking for a while, we paused and checked the pilot's foot. He was in considerable pain, and I was thankful for the rest, as I wasn't as strong as I'd thought, either. As we sat, we spotted a pair of civilians bicycling up the road toward us, each with a rifle slung over his shoulder. We waved them down, but they passed by, completely ignoring our presence, even though they could see that we had a wounded man with us. They continued on a short distance, then pulled over to the ditches

80 • PRISONER OF THE SWISS

on either side of the narrow road, abandoned their bikes, and lay down facing us, their rifles pointed directly at us.

We decided to approach them. As we did, they called out to us in French. Our co-pilot spoke some French, and told us they were asking for identification.

"We're American flyers," he told them in his broken French. "We just escaped from Switzerland and we're trying to get back to the American lines. We need immediate medical care for our pilot who has been shot through the foot during our escape."

After inspecting the foot, they put the pilot on one of the bikes and let us push him. One of our guards then walked in front, carrying his rifle, and the other brought up the rear with his rifle trained on our backs. We were taken to a small village about a mile down the road. By now it was dark—so dark we could not see as there were no streetlights in the town—and our pilot was in intense pain. We came to a warehouse and were led down a narrow flight of stairs, through a heavily curtained door, and into a dingy, ill-lit room filled with dirty Red Cross cots covered in dried blood. The giant room was held up by wooden posts, and everywhere you looked there were grubby, unshaven men—and a few women—staring at us, most with rifles or side arms.

They laid our pilot down and a man came in, took some supplies from a medical cabinet, and inspected the wound. Then, without any warning, he took a piece of cloth, twisted it into a tight ropelike coil, soaked it in iodine or something similar, inserted it in the entrance wound with an instrument like an ice pick, and pushed it all the way through the ankle so that it came out the exit wound. He then pulled the cloth back and forth inside the pilot's ankle, from one side to the other, and finally removed it. Whether because he was in shock or because he was so surprised, the pilot never uttered a sound. When it was over, he looked down at his ankle, now bandaged with a dirty rag, and said, "That was quick."

The other people in the room glared at us at first, but then began to act more friendly. One French man thought he knew English, and spoke to me rapid-fire, like a machine gun, so loudly I thought my ear drums would burst. I had no idea what he was saying, and after a while, he got very angry at me. In some of the only words I could understand, he told me that he didn't think I was really an American, because I couldn't understand English.

"You are in the hands of the Maquis," another man explained. "We had to be careful with you at first because many trapped Germans, and their French collaborators, are now trying to escape from the Allied advance. They dress as peasants to fool the Allies and us, and often they carry large amounts of money and valuables with them that they have stolen from the French people."

We stayed in this village for many days, waiting for it to be safe enough for an Air Force plane to fly in and pick us up. While we waited, quite a few other escapees filtered into the village, though we didn't see them all. We could hear the Allied planes flying over day and night, and the concussion of bombs not far off. Late one afternoon, we were told to assemble in a hurry at a large grassy field outside the village. To our surprise, we saw that all of our original crew—minus the bombardier—had made it to the village. A C-47 cargo plane came in low over the field, turned, and landed, taxiing hurriedly over to us, the engines roaring. As the plane moved slowly across the grass, a side door opened, a step came down, and we struggled aboard. As soon as the last man was in, the door was pulled shut, the engines went to full throttle, and we took off.

CHAPTER 12

The Return to England

We landed in England, close to Stone, which I was told was in Gloucestershire just east of the Bristol Channel. We straggled out of the C-47, clothed in our ill-fitting Resistance civilian clothing, looking filthy, ragged, and unshaven, and realized we were at a large air base that processed American airmen entering or leaving the European Theater.

First, they separated us by rank, with officers directed to one side of a giant room and enlisted men to the other. The room was filled with GIs sitting at tables pecking away on typewriters, each interrogating a soldier. When it was my turn, the clerk took my name, rank, and serial number, as well as my crew number, pilot's name, our group and squadron, and when and where I'd been shot down.

"I was shot down over Friedrichshafen, and then interned in Switzerland," I explained.

"How lucky can ya get," said the clerk, typing away, the first of many times I would be told this after mentioning my internment. It later got to the point where I no longer volunteered this information.

I was longing for some good old-fashioned Army chow and eating until I was fit to bust. It had been so long since I'd eaten a decent meal. But first, we had to get a physical, and mine brought shudders to the medic who checked me out. After stripping down to the waist, the medic took one look at my upper body, covered with festering boils and sores, and informed me that I would need a lot more treatment than they were equipped to give. He swabbed my worst sores with white, powdery

12. THE RETURN TO ENGLAND • 83

liquid and called a doctor to check me over. The doctor prescribed a hot bath, gave me some shots, and then cleared me for the mess hall.

By now, my stomach rumbled in protest and I rushed to the mess hall, only to find that since I did not have a mess kit, I would not be allowed to eat.

"You've got to be kidding me!" I told the GI serving the food.

"Why don't you have a mess kit?"

"I just escaped from Europe and returned to England today. I haven't had time to get issued a mess kit."

"No mess kit, no eat!" he repeated.

As I stood there, fuming, deciding whether or not to tear into somebody, a high-ranking officer strolled up and asked to be fed. He had no mess kit. The GI motioned to the back. "Head on into the kitchen, Colonel. They'll fix you up back there."

A captain now walked over. "Look Sergeant, there's nothing I can do. My orders are that anyone who doesn't have a mess kit and isn't in a special group, can't get fed."

"What about that colonel?" I asked, and added a few choice words.

"Sergeant, follow me," said the captain, leading me to his office in the kitchen, where he told me, "I don't like your attitude, and I intend to charge you with insubordination toward your superior officer and have you court-martialed. You won't be a sergeant after I'm through with you!"

All of a sudden, I began to cough—deep, racking coughs that sent stabs of pain through my body and made me forget about my empty stomach. I vomited up all the coagulated blood and everything else that had been rotting and fermenting in my shrunken stomach for days. Disgusted, the captain ordered an enlisted man to clean up the floor and turned to me angrily.

"You damned combat people think you're the only ones who go through hell," he stormed. "We folks back behind the lines go through just as much hell as you do, except we have it every single day!"

He ordered me to report immediately to my assigned quarters, without eating. In the barracks, I found my crew mates sacked out. After I'd reported, I returned to the cafeteria, and instead of being handed a tray, the captain handed me a rifle.

84 • PRISONER OF THE SWISS

"Sergeant, you should be damn glad I'm not taking your stripes," he told me. "Instead, you are going to do guard duty for the mess hall."

"Sir, could I at least eat first?"

"No mess kit, no food!"

Here I stood, in ratty civilian clothes, newly arrived in England and hungry as hell, and I was being given a rifle to pull guard duty of a mess hall. Incredible. I marched out back to the trash cans, opened the lids, and laid into the food that had been thrown away. Holding the rifle in one hand, I shoveled food into my mouth with the other, not caring what it was or who'd been eating it. I shoved food into my shriveled stomach until I vomited. Then I shoveled more in until I vomited again. Eventually, I was stuffed. I then pulled the rest of my guard duty, got a final warning that I'd be pulling it until I shipped out and that if I missed it I'd end up in the guard house, and then dropped, exhausted, on my bunk and fell into a deep sleep.

My medical treatment at the infirmary continued the following day. A doctor told me they'd need to admit me to the base hospital. Not only was he concerned that my sores would get infected, he was also very worried about my feet. I tried to tell him a little about my treatment in Switzerland, but he cut me off.

"You're imagining these things, Sergeant. The Swiss are neutral. Hell, they are the head of the Red Cross. They'd never treat anyone that way, not even a German, let alone an American."

"If you admit me, can I still get processed out with my buddies?"

"No. You'd have to stay behind."

"Then put some ointment on me and release me."

After they'd smeared on the ointment and wrapped my sores, the doctor told me that the Army was now flying former POWs directly to the States. The military hospitals in Europe were clogged with injured men, and I'd be getting better treatment stateside anyway. In the two days before we shipped out, I pulled guard duty at the mess hall, and on the second day was finally issued clothing and a damn mess kit.

Before shipping out, my pilot found out about my treatment and went to the mess hall with our navigator. He gave the officer a piece of his mind, tempering it because the captain outranked him. He also reported the

12. THE RETURN TO ENGLAND • 85

incident to the base commander, but I doubt anything came of it. When I think of how the officers on our crew stood up for us, such as the time when the operations officer wanted to steal our sleeping bags, all I can say is we had the best officers anyone could have ever hoped to serve with. It rankles me to know that they returned to the States with much lower ranks because of their loyalty to us enlisted men. Each time I encountered this moronic type of behavior from superiors later in civilian life, it brought back memories of those days, that officer, and those sleeping bags.

We walked back onto our old base at Shipdham a short time later, and into our old Quonset hut. The base seemed strange. In our hut, we tried to find the personal items we'd left behind. We'd bought presents for our families and had plenty of things we hadn't taken on our final mission like books, letters, and photos.

To a man, we didn't find a single thing. It was as if we'd never existed, at least not at the 66th Squadron. We were told everything had been shipped home to our families. We looked for our bicycle. Again to no avail.

There wasn't a single friendly face in the entire squadron. It might have been my imagination, but the men of the 66th now seemed different from the ones we'd known. And the old, beat-up, mean-looking camouflaged B-24s were all gone—replaced by shiny, new, polished aluminum ones. The crews wore fancy new protection gear that hadn't existed when we flew our missions—things like flak vests and helmets. Their flight suits looked new.

Ours looked like they'd been in the Civil War. Even though it hadn't been that long, we were already relics of the past, our bombing days long over, and the friendships we'd forged with the other crews of the 44th Bomb Group had vanished like mist. Some of our friends had perished, others were prisoners, and many more had simply gone home. It was a different war now, fought by younger men, and our part in it was over. Though I'd hated the war, everything about it—the constant fear of injury, imprisonment or death, being away from my family—this was a tough realization. Once a soldier has gone through hell with his old friends, and there is nothing left but memories, no friendship seems to come as easily or be as deeply satisfying. You can never go back, and your present and future will always be measured against this sense of loss.

CHAPTER 13

Interrogation in London

We went to London, where we were given new uniforms, new medals, and put up in a fancy hotel. My enjoyment was tempered considerably when I got my back pay owed me for the time I'd been imprisoned in Switzerland. The U.S. government paid for every month I was interned—four months in all—but did not pay me a nickel for the time I had spent during my escape, or my time in prison. I was informed that I was classified as AWOL—absent without leave—during these periods and not eligible for pay.

Each of us was placed alone in a small room with an interrogator from Army Intelligence—known at the time as the OSS (Office of Strategic Service)—the precursor to the CIA. The interrogating officers had been trained in how to extract every useful bit of information. Their interrogation method was different from that used after a combat mission, where we sat down and were interrogated as a crew. Here, all questioning was conducted one-on-one, then the interrogators cross-checked their extracted information for commonalities and discrepancies before a separate interrogator would weave all the accounts into a common story that was the closest approximation to the truth.

My interrogation lasted days. Of particular interest was what kinds of aircraft I had seen on each mission, when we had seen new types, and the evolution of German fighter strategies. Every time the officer felt the questioning was becoming tiring, he dismissed me and I could spend the rest of the day sightseeing in London.

The interrogation took a harsh turn one day when the interrogator noticed that I was uncomfortable and agitated when alone in a room with him when the door was closed. Up to this point, I had avoided specifics about Wauwilermoos. I explained to him, in general terms, that I had been held prisoner at a Swiss prison called Wauwilermoos after my escape attempt and had some unpleasant experiences there.

He shot me a puzzled look. "Wauwilermoos? I've never heard of it before."

I told him a little about it. He claimed he'd never heard of the prison or its commandant. The OSS knew nothing of the place. Shocked, I decided to give him some basic information.

"Will you record everything I say about Wauwilermoos, if I tell you about it?" I asked beforehand.

"Of course," he assured me. "Everything you say will be placed before the International War Crimes Commission, if it's considered inhuman treatment, and also in your own Army Air Force records, regardless of the nature of the treatment."

"When I return to the States," I told the officer, "I intend to tell every American newspaper that will listen about how I was mistreated by the Swiss and how I was forsaken by the American attaché in Bern, simply for trying to do what every soldier is ordered to do when captured—return to his own lines."

As I told him, the officer studiously jotted copious notes. Soon, however, I noticed that he had stopped writing and asked him about it. He told me he intended to write it down later. This upset me. He became more and more upset as I told the story, at times seeming almost as unsettled as I was. He then terminated the session, telling me to return to my quarters and report back the following day at a specific time.

I arrived a half-hour early, anxious to be done because I had a date with a girl I'd met in London, and because our crew was preparing to depart for the States. To my surprise, there were two men in the interrogation room—the original officer and a second man, a captain with an Eighth Air Force patch on his shoulder. He also wore a gold cross on his lapels, and was introduced as a chaplain and minister of the Church of the Brethren, the same church to which I belonged.

88 • PRISONER OF THE SWISS

We sat down, and the lieutenant handed the captain a sheaf of papers covering my confinement at Wauwilermoos. As he read, the captain shook his head. When he finished, he looked me directly in the eyes and said, "I don't believe this statement to be true."

The Swiss, he explained, were a gentle, caring people, and our own Church of the Brethren had many Swiss adherents.

"Have you talked to any Swiss people since the war started?" I asked him. He admitted he hadn't.

"People and nations sometimes change dramatically in wartime," I told him. "Every nation has good and bad people, and it just so happens most of these bad people managed to worm their way into positions of authority."

Undeterred, he proclaimed that there was no such place as Wauwilermoos. I dug into my wallet and pulled out the scrap of paper given me after my trial in Bern. It had my name and it, as well as the name of the prison I'd been sent to, Wauwilermoos. Both men were surprised to see I still had this paper. The interrogator reached for it, and they read it over together several times.

"We'll need to keep this for your file," said the captain.

"I've gone through hell for that piece of paper!" I protested. "No one is going to take it from me!" Amazingly, he handed it back, and I put it in my wallet. Seeing the paper entirely changed the tone of the meeting. Both men now treated me with respect and courtesy. They excused themselves for several minutes, telling me to go get a bite to eat and then to report back when I was done; they had to do some checking with their superiors.

After I ate, the original interrogator and myself went to a different room. I was relieved that the chaplain was gone, but noted that the interrogator seemed nervous, as if he were waiting for someone. The room was quiet as a tomb. When the door opened, the captain walked in shouting, "Attention!" The interrogator and I jumped to our feet, and a spit-and-polish full colonel with the flaming sword of the OSS on his shoulder strode in.

The colonel indicated that the other two men could sit, but that I was to remain at full attention. He picked up a sheaf of papers, shook

13 · INTERROGATION IN LONDON · 89

them at me, and spoke: "Sergeant, you are a Goddamned liar! There is no such place as Wauwilermoos in Switzerland, and if there was, the Swiss wouldn't put an American soldier there for nothing more than an attempted escape! If you were thrown into a Swiss federal prison, your crime must have been something much worse than what you claim! We know that the interned American airmen are held in resort hotels, with the best food, and treated like kings. The American government is paying the Swiss large sums of money to care for you. If you disobeyed the American military attaché, you would have been punished by the Americans, not the Swiss."

I attempted to speak but was rebuffed. As he continued his harangue, I became more and more angry and afraid. When his rant was done, I was given permission to speak. Unfortunately, all I could do was cough uncontrollably. I had nowhere to throw up the blood and phlegm, and had no choice but to cough it up into my service cap.

As they watched me with a mixture of horror and concern, I tore off my jacket and shirt, exposing my flaming boils and sores. I then pulled down my pants and showed them the boils that festered below my waistline. I took off my shoes, and showed them my frostbitten blackened feet. "Do I look like a prisoner who has been treated humanely by his captors?" I asked.

"Give me your papers," said the colonel. I felt I had no alternative. The lieutenant took them. The colonel turned brusquely to the lieutenant. "Destroy them."

He proceeded to explain why the matter was being handled in this way. Apparently, Air Force bombers from the United States had bombed Switzerland on several occasions, leading to a substantial loss of life and damage of property. The American government was currently negotiating a settlement for these incidents, and the damages were expected to run into the tens of millions of dollars. The head of the OSS in Bern did not want any bad press to get back to the American people and hold up the negotiations. I was therefore being put under a gag order.

My statement about talking to the press had been a terrible mistake, one that could cost me dearly. If I hadn't said it, I would be enjoying my last few days in London before my happy return to the United States.

The colonel warned me that if I were to press on with this report, I would be classified by the Army as mentally unstable and given a Section Eight discharge. A Section Eight meant they could put me in an Army or veterans' hospital for years. I had no doubts that they were fully prepared to carry out these threats.

Nothing about my imprisonment at Wauwilermoos, or any other treatment I received in Switzerland, ever made it into my files. My discharge papers didn't even mention that I had been a Swiss internee. To further complicate matters, my military records, including all my medical reports, were destroyed in a huge fire at the VA warehouse in St. Louis a few years later. It was as if I had spent the years 1942 to 1945 in the U.S. Army Air Force doing absolutely nothing.

I had not mentioned to the colonel, when he confiscated my Wauwilermoos paper, that I had given him a copy. I still had the original. I do to this day. But not having the rest of my actual records would come back to haunt me many times in my life.

CHAPTER 14

Home Again

At first our crew thought we might be sent back to the States on one of the many ships bringing troops and supplies to Europe. I'd always wanted to ride on a giant ocean liner. However, military policy stipulated that all ex-POWs, evadees, and internees would be flown home. On November 1, 1944, our entire crew—minus the bombardier—boarded a four-engine C-54 transport plane filled with American service personnel at a base outside of London. As we left the coast behind, I think we all felt the same emotions. First, immense relief that we had survived the war. Second, pride that we had done our part to bring about what we hoped would be the fall of fascism in Europe. Finally, a deep sense of sadness, as we saw in our mind's eyes the faces of many young men, our friends, who had flown with us and fought with us but would never be going home. Some of them were never found, and their families didn't even have the closure of a body to bury and visit. All they would have would be a simple marker over an empty plot of soil.

We arrived in New York City on November 4, 1944, passing almost directly over the Statue of Liberty's welcoming torch. It seemed decades, not a few years, since we'd last seen our homeland at Presque Isle, Maine. That night we were feted as heroes at a New York nightclub, and patrons bought our drinks and our dinner. We imbibed until we could barely stand, then retired for the night at a processing center of returning Army Air Force personnel.

The next morning, I was given a complete physical, and the doctor showed great concern over my wounds, the operation on my rectum in particular. He wanted to know who did the operation, but with the dire warning of the OSS officer echoing in my head, I told him it was a combat wound for which I'd been treated at a Swiss hospital.

"Switzerland?" commented the doctor. "How lucky can you get!"

Each day, the medical staff put me in a hot sitz bath, pouring medicine into the bath continually. Afterwards, they slathered me with gray paste and wrapped my wounds with gauze bandages. This seemed to pull out the infection. They did the same with my frostbitten feet, putting stockings over them after wrapping. The doctors told me that the healing process would take about a month, perhaps a little more—disappointing because the rest of the crew was preparing for their 30-day leaves to visit their families. My desire to see my mother, and to get home, was so strong that it over-rode my good sense, and I begged to be released from the hospital so that I could go home, promising to treat my wounds myself when I got there. The facility was packed with patients, and more showed up every day, so it didn't take long to get my way.

Syracuse looked the same. I ate a big breakfast with my sister and her family in town. My brother-in-law drove me out to the house on the hill where I'd grown up. Everyone was excited to see me reunited with my mother, and also curious to see if Toby would remember me. I'd had Toby since I was seven, and had to really fight to keep him. My unemployed stepfather, who never had much to do with putting food on the table, didn't want to feed him, and he made me promise that I'd buy all Toby's food myself.

Fifteen months earlier, when I'd been home on leave, Toby had remembered me after an hour or so. I was sure he'd remember me this time.

Mother and Toby met me coming up the lane. I ran to Mother and we held each other tight. Toby, thinking I was trying to hurt her, latched onto my pant leg and bit me. Though disappointed in his reaction, it was understandable. Mom and I talked for hours, and I tried everything to get on Toby's good side, but he kept his distance, growling every time I attempted to touch him. I felt bad, and Mother felt worse, but we

14. HOME AGAIN • 93

both knew that three years is a long time in an animal's memory despite our long history together. Though Toby eventually came around, I was never sure if he remembered me or if he saw me as a new friend; we were never as close again.

I then went out to the barn to see the car I'd bought just before going into the service and stored lovingly in the back of the barn, jacked up to keep the tires off the ground. I'd even draped flannel bedsheets over her, to keep the dust from setting on her paint. Before I'd left, I'd told her, "Sleep tight, my beauty. I'll return as soon as we defeat the enemy."

When I opened the barn door, all I saw was my brother's Chevy. My car was gone. I walked back to the house, spread my arms jokingly, and asked my mother, "Okay, where is it?" At this, Mother broke down and sobbed uncontrollably.

"After the town heard you were shot down over Germany and missing in action, everyone pestered me to sell your car," she said tearfully. "I told them all, 'No, that's Dan's car' and everyone accepted that except for one man, a mechanic in Syracuse. He told me that if you were a POW, you wouldn't be home for years, if ever, and by then the car would be rusted, the tires would be rotten, and the engine would be worthless. He told me that he was doing you a favor by buying it now, while it still had value." Mother had co-signed for it, so all she had to do was sign to sell it to the mechanic. He paid her a fraction of what it was worth in after-war prices, and less than half what I had paid for it.

I spent the first week of leave in bed. Mother changed the sheets every day, mixing and applying her own concoctions to my wounds. She then put a hot towel over them and the next morning it had drawn out the poison so I could hardly tell where they had been. She made other potions, which I drank. Some were quite vile.

The last 20 days of my leave were spent on a 1936 Harley-Davidson motorcycle that I bought to replace the lost Ford. Before leaving again, I gave Mother explicit instructions not to sell it until two years after the war was over, and then only if I didn't return.

CHAPTER 15

Endings

I reported to C-46 Commando Aircraft Engineering School in Buffalo, feeling fairly healed up. The school was small, and military discipline was lax. During the six-week course, I didn't have any access to medical care, but continued treating my boils and feet with the ointment issued me upon arrival in New York City. Many of the other students in the class were also ex-combat veterans, but while I looked forward to getting thorough training so that I could find a job in the aircraft industry after the war, most of the other guys goofed off, just putting in time until their discharges.

After graduation, I was sent to West Palm Beach, Florida, riding first class from snow drifts to palm trees. The new base was a large overhaul maintenance repair depot, responsible for upkeep on the C-54 four-engine cargo transport planes used in North Africa and the Italian campaign. After each plane had reached its maximum flight time, it was sent to our base for a complete overhaul. Though I'd trained to repair the C-46, I had enough all-around background in aircraft maintenance that the switch was easy, and I was rapidly assigned as a ground crew chief, in charge of my own ground crew and responsible for a specific aircraft. Our job was to take each beat-up, combat-weary airplane and restore it to as near like-new condition as possible—not an easy task.

I spent my off-duty time with the base's civilian employees, learning all I could about the C-54 and its maintenance procedures, and before long was promoted to line chief, where I made many suggestions that sped up the overhauls. The engineering officer, a captain, assured me that I'd have a great future in the post-war Air Force. In addition to my regular pay, I earned flight pay because I went up on each post-overhaul check flight as the qualified flight engineer.

It was during one routine check flight, as the pilot took the plane up to altitude, that I suddenly began coughing severely, then vomited blood and phlegm. The pilot aborted, we landed, and the next thing I remember I was lying in a hospital bed, on oxygen and under quarantine. My bed was covered with cloth netting, the hair on my head and body had been shaved off, and I was smeared with salve.

An Army nurse came in, wearing a mask. "Why haven't you reported your condition to us?" she scolded. "And why were you attempting to fly with your lungs in such bad shape? How long have you had tuberculosis?"

"I was a prisoner of war," I answered groggily. "I got sick overseas."

She picked up the chart at the foot of my bed. "This doesn't mention you being a prisoner of war. In fact, your medical records are completely nonexistent." She did a double take. "It's strange," she said, "that the only records of any kind are your induction immunizations, records of your schooling in the States, and your assignment to the 44th Bomb Group." Though I didn't tell the nurse anything about Switzerland, the doctor performing the follow-up exam the next day was convinced I had been through a major ordeal to be in such poor health.

"I can't help you unless you tell me exactly where you were and what happened," he warned.

"I can't do that, sir. I am under direct orders never to tell anyone, under threat of court-martial, either how I received my injuries, or what country I was in when I received them."

"I find that very hard to believe," he said.

"May I return to the maintenance department once I get better?"

"Absolutely not! Not for a very long time—if ever. There will be no more flying with those lungs. I'm taking you off flying status effective immediately."

My treatment continued. I remained wary of men, and hated to be in a room behind closed doors with them, especially with only one.

96 • PRISONER OF THE SWISS

This situation came to a head when a new orderly began administering the baths. He was a male orderly but acted feminine, and at one point, attempted to show me how to wash myself. This literally sent me flying out of the tub, and I pushed him through a thick metal door, tearing it completely off its hinges. It took a small army and a loaded syringe to subdue me, and when I woke up, I found myself in a room with bars on the windows. The staff brought in a psychiatrist to try to figure out what was wrong with me emotionally, but other than telling him I had been treated badly in a foreign prison, I kept to my end of the agreement with the OSS officer.

A few weeks later, as I watched a movie at a theater near my new posting in Montgomery, Alabama, the screen went dark and the public address system began playing "God Bless America" and announced that the Japanese had surrendered and the war was over at last.

My new job was pleasant, driving OCS recruits around the base, and I definitely wanted to stay in the service long enough for my records to catch up to me, so that I could get the proper pay and medical care I needed. My sores continued to fester and my feet were still not properly healed. I also wanted to make sure that the TB virus had been eradicated from my system before exiting the military. I signed papers reenlisting and even applied for Officer Candidate School.

Instead, I found my name on a shortlist of men designated for immediate discharge. I appealed to the OCS major, my boss, and he found that the order to discharge me had come from Washington, D.C. and there was no appeal. His demeanor changed from supportive to dismissive after the order. Quickly, and without a chance for either an exit physical or an appeal, I was mustered out. It seemed that my willingness to serve my country had been received with open arms, but I was now an undesirable burden because of what had happened to me in Switzerland. Unlike many veterans who never served in combat but figured out how to get disability benefits—some of whom received the full 100 percent—I joined a large group of combat veterans who had legitimate claims but never got to file because they were discouraged from doing so by the very administration that was supposed to be helping them. This saved the American government billions of dollars in honest claims.

Sadly, most of the veterans bilked out of their disability have long since passed away. The ones who are left, and who are trying to rectify things, are now met with the question, "Why didn't you try to do this sooner?" We are looked at as people who are trying to get something we do not deserve.

I went back to Syracuse and got my pre-war job at Macy's marina on Lake Wawasee, still run by the same husband and his wife. The pay was low, the work menial. Nothing was said about the war, except when the owner told me how lucky I was to have flown air combat early in the war, before the invasion when the air war got dangerous (quite the opposite was true). Or when he told me how lucky I'd been to get shot down and end up in Switzerland. He'd heard we'd been treated like royalty by the Swiss.

I would spend my days building metal boats and rebuilding speed boats. He took me to a large shed filled with tons of new galvanized sheet metal that we would use to build the boats.

"I thought all that metal had to be turned in for the war effort," I commented, eying his stash.

He winked at me. "Funny, I hadn't heard about that."

He showed me another store room filled with dozens of Evinrude outboard motors, brand new and still in their crates, as well as a large number of covered, brand-new Chris-Craft speed boats.

He'd bought all these at pre-war rock-bottom prices, and had sat on them so that he could sell them in the post-war boom. The man was going to make a fortune from the war—the same man who'd just told me how lucky I'd been to fight in it.

The last straw was another comment he made one of my first days back. "I don't want you to sit around all day telling war stories. The war must be forgotten. Now it's working time." That was it. Without saying a word, I got on my Harley and put as many miles between him and me as I could. I could not erase from my mind the millions of men, women, and children who had died all over the world or who were crippled for life for nothing more than to make this greedy American bastard rich.

CHAPTER 16

The Black Hole of Wauwilermoos Returns

My time in Wauwilermoos left me with a permanent companion. Though not tangible in the normal sense, it stalked me everywhere I went, sabotaging my chances for a normal reentry into civilian life. His name was fear, and he reared his ugly head every time I was in an enclosed area with men I didn't know. Nowadays, this would be seen as Post Traumatic Stress Disorder, but in 1945, there was no such thing, only a vague understanding that traumatic experiences in combat could cause emotional damage. PTSD causes nightmares, flashbacks, blackouts, and bizarre waking behavior triggered by certain stimuli. Even now, 70 years later, I suffer its relentless attacks.

The first manifestation occurred when I reacted to the male orderly, and the results could have been tragic; fortunately, no one was hurt and I didn't get in trouble. The first occasion in civilian life happened within months of my return home to Indiana. Though I had a guaranteed job at the marina, I wasn't thrilled at working for starvation wages for someone who had been a war profiteer. It happened that my brother-in-law from Mishawaka—a sister city of South Bend—had been working in a factory there for many years, and he informed me that they had lots of prime openings in manufacturing. During the war, the factory had constructed fuel cells for my beloved B-24 bomber, and it was shifting to peacetime production and seeking qualified applicants, especially former servicemen.

16. THE BLACK HOLE RETURNS • 99

I showed up at the factory at 7 a.m., filled out the application, and went for my physical. A nurse ushered me into a small room with a straight-backed chair and a cot and told me to completely disrobe and wait for the doctor. I hadn't expected this, and was worried what the doctor would think when he saw my scars. As I sat there, I was suddenly no longer in the innocuous factory office, but in Wauwilermoos, or Lucerne, or the interrogation room in London. Each nightmarish place flashed into my brain like a bolt of lightning. I felt trapped, suffocated, as if the walls were beginning to push inwards, and I jumped up naked and pushed on the door. It was locked from the outside, to prevent others from entering. I pounded feverishly on the door until the nurse unlocked it, and when I tried to get out, she quickly shut it again and locked it, assuring me no one would hurt me. I began to calm down. Security showed up. I got dressed and escaped from the factory as fast as I could.

I was now sitting on the side of a road. I was on my Harley. I checked my gas gauge. Out of gas. Where was I? I had no idea. How had I gotten here? Again, no clue. I was on the outskirts of a small village. I was wearing my military uniform, the same one I'd worn to my interview, since none of my civilian clothes fit me. I pushed my Harley down the strange road until I came to a service station and fueled up.

"Where am I?" I asked the attendant. "How do I get to South Bend?"

"On the same road you came on," he told me.

I explained that I didn't know how I had got here, and had no idea how to get home. He looked at my uniform, and all the medals on it, and patriotically gave me directions.

When I got back to my sister and brother-in-law's house, my brother-in-law had just come home from work, where he'd heard all about the commotion, and he told me that I'd not only made a fool out of myself, but out of him as well. I climbed on my Harley and rode through the night, back to the house I grew up in, the house where my childhood had ended four years ago, where my mother waited for me, and my dog Toby. I got home in the wee hours of the morning, while the world slept, and there was Toby, waiting for his new friend—the guy he didn't remember had raised him from a scruffy little ball of newly weaned fluff.

We walked together to the edge of the gravel pit that took up half the farm and sat down, looking up at millions of twinkling stars.

As a boy, I'd talked to Toby to clear my head and ease my troubles. Tonight, I did the same. I thought of the many things that had happened since I'd left this peaceful spot such a short time ago. The war was over, but at the same time, it wasn't. Not for me. It would never be over. I knew that now. The war was embedded deep in my mind, in every dark corner of my subconscious. Could I ever really get past it? Or would I forever be trapped in the black hole of Wauwilermoos?

CHAPTER 17

Appendix to the Original 1995 Edition of *The Black Hole of Wauwilermoos*

It wasn't until 45 years after the war that I found out that my bombardier had not gotten out of Switzerland that day we were separated on the train platform. Instead, he had been sent to Wauwilermoos. After serving several weeks there, he and several other Americans bribed Béguin to allow them to escape, made it to France, then to England and America. I felt it was my fault he'd been captured, and when we met at the 44th Bomb Group Reunion in Dayton in 1988 I apologized. We decided it was probably for the best, as he could have been killed in the hail of gunfire during our escape over the barbed wire into France.

André Béguin was put on trial after the war by the Swiss government. During the trial it was determined that Béguin was indeed a member of the Swiss Nazi Party. His sadistic nature was proven by written and oral testimony at trial, and the Swiss were surprised that someone of his bent had ever been allowed to administer a prison camp. He was accused of using money earmarked for the day-to-day operations of the camp for his own benefit, including the support of his mistresses. This meant that prisoners went without food, medical care, and other basic necessities.

It seemed strange to me that the Swiss tried Béguin for misusing money, and didn't try him for destroying human lives. It also seemed strange to me that Switzerland, the headquarters of the International

Red Cross, would not allow foreign prisoners at Wauwilermoos to receive Red Cross parcels or to be visited by a Red Cross representative.

In 1994, I was invited to return to Switzerland, and was given a personal apology by then–President Kaspar Villiger, both in writing and in person. The letter states in part:

> I received your account of the experience you made during your internment in Switzerland as a member of the U.S. Armed Forces from the Swiss Embassy in Washington. I read your portrayal with great interest and regret that your memory of your internment in 1944, and in particular, that of your detention in Wauwilermoos is colored by such traumatic experience. I appreciate that it is difficult for you to understand why you were assigned to the Wauwilermoos detention camp. Together with innumerable other young Americans, you came to Europe to rescue the continent from fascist aggressors ... Your attempt to flee and rejoin your unit was not defamatory, though such behavior was in fact contrary to Swiss orders ... From today's point of view, the Swiss military punished you very severely ... This sentence reflects the important pressure exercised by other countries on Switzerland which was then surrounded by war. The Swiss authorities were afraid that a less severe attitude towards attempts of interned military personnel to escape would be interpreted as preferential treatment by the other warring party.

In late October, 1995, my wife Betty and I visited Switzerland. The trip was paid for by a Swiss news station that smelled a good story. It soon became apparent after our arrival that we were being used by the media for their own purposes with little regard for my mental or physical health.

The first stop was Adelboden, a place that brought back both good and bad memories. We found the same bus I had used to make my escape in 1944, and we completely reenacted it for the cameras. However, the press of the cameras and the onlookers began to bother my claustrophobia. At Frutigen, I was placed in my old cell for the cameras, a surprise I could very much have done without. I collapsed while the cameras rolled.

That night I was plagued by terrifying nightmares. The next day we were scheduled to go to Wauwilermoos. I no longer wished to continue, but felt obligated because the news company had paid for my expenses. The actual prison had been destroyed by the Swiss right after the war, and a drug treatment center had been built on the spot. I was interviewed by a local news reporter from Wauwil. It was a harsh interview during which he refused to believe that there had been a prison there or a commandant named Béguin. His open hostility was unnerving. Just like the German civilians around the Nazi death camps later denied knowledge of the camps' existence or purpose, so the citizens around Wauwilermoos denied its existence.

On October 30, Betty and I met with President Villiger, the most pleasant and sincere person I had ever met. Everything he said came from his heart.

On July 30, 1996, more than 50 years after the war ended, I was awarded the Prisoner of War Medal, the first of the Wauwilermoos survivors to receive it. All but one of the rest would have to wait until 2014. I also received the Distinguished Flying Cross for my efforts to keep our plane in the air before landing in Switzerland. The ceremony was held at Tucson's Davis–Monthan Air Force Base. Never in my wildest dreams had I expected this day to ever come. It went a long way toward healing some of my bitter feelings.

The ball had started rolling around 1990, when I finally received therapy for Post Traumatic Stress Disorder at the Tucson VA Medical Center. As part of my therapy, I wrote my book, *The Black Hole of Wauwilermoos*. Air Force Chief of Staff General Ronald Fogleman read the book and proceeded to verify its contents. In a statement from Washington, General Fogleman said: "I am pleased the Air Force could award these two decorations after all these years."

The general presenting the award, Lt. Gen. James F. Record, commander of the Twelfth Air Force at Davis–Monthan, told me, "This today is the story of Dan Culler and the chance to recognize his heroic actions in World War II."

In addition to the Prisoner of War Medal, Lt. Gen. Record presented me with the Distinguished Flying Cross for my efforts on our 25th and final mission to keep our airplane in the air long enough to make it to Dübendorf. Though I still feel I was just doing the job I'd been trained to do, the general thanked me for "bravery, courage, exemplary knowledge and skills under extremely hazardous conditions. In disregard for his own personal safety, he was able to make an emergency fuel transfer and put out the fire and kept his plane flying until they could make a safe emergency landing. In doing so, he helped save the lives of his crew members."

It was a ceremony dedicated to healing, and I found some of my deep anger and heartbreak toward the Army dissipating. I also realized that if I could do it all over again, I would not try to escape from Switzerland. My indoctrination had ingrained in me the importance of escape, but I doubt I would be as gung-ho now.

I owe most of my recovery to my wife Betty, who has never left my side in all the years I've suffered. She has held me in her arms many nights after I've awakened from a terrible flashback. When she passed away a few years ago, I was heartbroken, and unsure if I could go on, but I have.

I know I'll never heal, never truly escape from the hell of Wauwilermoos. Nor will I understand why human beings can be so incredibly evil. I'll never understand it, but I know it to be true. There is much evil in this world, and much good. That's just the way the world is.

We each must walk life's circle of thorns. My belief is that no matter what pitfalls, hardships, and physical and mental abuse a person faces in life, they can rise above self-pity. It is our responsibility to continue living our lives in such a way that we can be a credit to our family, our community, our country, and our planet. Each of us comes into the world with different abilities to manage physical and mental pain. Some poor souls, handicapped beyond belief, overcome it and turn it around to their betterment. Others with healthy bodies and minds throw away everything, living their lives blaming one bad experience for every failure. It's common in our society today to blame others for our own lack of success. We can blame the government, or big business, or any of a number of eligible scapegoats, but we as individuals must rise above whatever it is that tries to bring us down, and just maybe our strength will prevail and bring change to our great land.

Not all men are destined for great success. In fact, some are doomed to fail no matter what they do. There is no sin in failure; the sin is in giving up. With the time I have left, I will continue to move toward that thin ray of light shining through the dark clouds. Whether or not I reach that light is entirely in my hands.

I have walked the circle of thorns. It has been a hard walk, the irony being that unless one makes it, he will never know true compassion for others. A person who has walked the circle of thorns and is still able to love and forgive will find peace and control his own destiny.

Finally, it takes no wisdom or courage to hate and kill, but it takes much wisdom and courage to love and make peace. Writing this book has brought me a semblance of peace. It is my hope that each person who reads it will learn the importance of forgiveness in the healing process, and also will have learned of a little-known and painful footnote in the story of the most terrible war mankind has ever known.

Part II
Aftermath

Rob Morris and Dwight S. Mears

CHAPTER 18

Moving On

Dan went on to live a successful life, meeting each obstacle with the same gritty determination he showed as a prisoner of war in Wauwilermoos. He got married to his wife Betty, had three children, and spent a career in the trucking industry, putting his mechanical and logistical skills to good use. He retired to Arizona, to a suburb of Tucson, and found that the Arizona air did wonders for his residual tuberculosis.

In December of 2000, Dan received one of the most unusual and unexpected Christmas cards ever sent. It carried a Swiss stamp and postmark. Opening it up, he read the following:

Dear Mr. Dan Culler,

I learnt your story and the hard trials you went through. They make my heart bleed, awfully bleed, because I am youngest daughter of Captain André Béguin and I'm born on the eve of my father's lawsuit (17-2-1946). After so many sufferings for everyone of us, for you, for my sister and for my father took, after so many sufferings …

I BEG YOUR PARDON

And with the most sincerity, I send you all my best wishes for better health, a Merry and peaceful Christmas and a Happy New Year.

God Bless you,
Jacqueline-André Perissinott

CHAPTER 19

André Béguin and General Barnwell Rhett Legge

Additional information about the trial of Wauwilermoos commandant André Béguin reveals a troubled man with a troubling past. As stated, Béguin was a Swiss Nazi, a member of the National Front, known to wear a Nazi uniform and sign his correspondence with "Heil Hitler!" He had been dismissed from the Swiss Army in 1937 for financial fraud and various encounters with the police.

Béguin's trial lasted 149 days. He was convicted of administrative demeanors, dishonoring the Swiss and their army, embezzlement, and withholding complaints from inmates. In its decision, the court described Béguin as a "crook, embezzler, conman and inhuman." He was sentenced to several years in prison, fined, and stripped of his rights.

The American military attaché, General Barnwell Legge, is a bit more enigmatic. He comes across in Dan Culler's memoirs as a lazy, unconcerned man who turns his back on the needs of the American internees. In fact, the truth is more complex, and goes a long way toward vindicating General Legge historically.

According to American historian Dwight Mears:

> Of all of the internees I spoke with, very few liked him. This includes those who had to work with him directly, such as Captain McGuire, who for a time was the ranking internee in one of the camps. Many made disparaging remarks about him, and believed that he was working directly against their interests by refusing to assist with escape attempts or to intervene on their behalf after those

19. ANDRÉ BÉGUIN AND GENERAL BARNWELL RHETT LEGGE • 111

attempts failed. The truth was more nuanced, because Legge was actually overall in charge of the escape network, and was coordinating this with the OSS, which was entirely unknown to most of the internees. He did not have direct access to many of the internees due to their diverse sequestration in the mountains, and I think he didn't want it widely known among the internment commission that he was directing the escapes (hence the public directive that appeared to say that nobody should attempt escape, which was an unsuccessful attempt to manage the escapes and improve their chances of success).

The Swiss eventually discovered the Legation's efforts, and considered expelling some of the officials (they noticed the pattern of escapes immediately after contact by Legation authorities, as well as the brazen transport of escaping internees via official staff cars, etc.). The Swiss actively impeded U.S. efforts to contact the internees, mainly because they knew that the officials were providing money and information on escape contacts. As a result, most of the internees had absolutely no idea that the escape network existed, and this is why many of them struck out on their own. Often they only received help from the Legation after an unsuccessful escape attempt, since this raised their priority in the eyes of the Legation because they were now facing extended mistreatment in a punishment facility.

It is also important to credit Legge with unwavering advocacy for the internees who were punished for escaping. When Swiss officials failed to heed his concerns about Wauwilermoos, Legge threatened to leak the matter to the press and involve American diplomats. Legge threatened in a letter to Swiss Internment Commissioner Dolfuss: "[Conditions in Wauwilermoos] will certainly be harmful to Swiss-American relations when this entire matter comes into the light." Legge further stated that "your [Switzerland's] splendid national traditions of service to belligerent nations is world-renowned and I am sure that a just criticism of treatment of these internees whom the fortunes of war find within your borders, would be painful to the public conscience." He claimed that the Americans "believed they were in a friendly neutral country," but due to Wauwilermoos "they are now convinced that they are being treated with injustice and discrimination." Legge informed Dolfuss that "it would not appear just that men who have been guilty only of the honorable offence of endeavouring to rejoin their forces" should be punished the same as soldiers of other nationalities "who are being punished for misdemeanors, drunkenness, insubordination and kindred offenses." He informed Dolfuss that "regardless of any repressive measures taken, our aviators will continue to attempt to escape." He warned that "I cannot too strongly recommend [paroling the Americans] as a prompt if only temporary solution to the Wauwilermoos situation before the storm which is brewing breaks." He reminded Dolfuss that "our military chiefs in Washington are seriously concerned about these matters."

Legge followed through with Minister Harrison, who cabled the State Department and obtained an official protest from the acting secretary in November 1944. The protest led the Swiss foreign minister, Pilet-Golaz, to pressure Defense Minister Karl Kobelt to release the American and Commonwealth internees from Wauwilermoos. Dolfuss did so, and resigned as internment commissioner on the same day (but continued in his duties as Swiss Army adjutant general). Legge made good on his threat to leak the matter to the press, as his protest to the internment commission was quoted nearly verbatim in an article published in the August 1945 edition of *Yank, the Army Weekly*.

Legge also defended the honor of the internees when Gen. Arnold heeded the false rumors about bomber crews defecting to neutral countries in the summer of 1944. He wrote to Gen. Arnold that the alleged morale problems were "practically nonexistent here," and that "I know of none who is not ready and willing to fight again." He claimed that "[I] believe you have only cause to feel proud of your command as I am," and that "my greatest trouble here is preventing them from trying to escape."

According to historian Dwight Mears, "even though the unilateral escapes ran contrary to Legge's attempts to direct successful escapes himself, scuttled negotiations over an exchange with Germany, embarrassed the Swiss authorities, and jeopardized the status of the U.S. Legation staff, he realized that the escape attempts were probably inevitable and ultimately honorable in motive."

CHAPTER 20

Recognition at Last

Dwight Mears was a young West Point cadet when he noticed the pair of cracked leather shoes at his grandmother's house. The shoes were nearly worn through the soles, and he couldn't imagine why she had kept them. She replied that she'd never throw them away. They were the very shoes that her late husband, Mears's grandfather, Army Air Force Lt. George W. Mears, had worn during his escape from Switzerland in World War II. He'd walked many miles in those shoes, through Switzerland and then France, before finally meeting up with American forces near Annecy. His grandmother knew little else of the story, except that he'd been interned there after his B-17 Flying Fortress, "Superball," was shot down during a mission to Munich in March 1944.

"My grandfather was wounded," recounts Mears. "His controls were shot away and he'd lost two engines, but he managed to fly the crippled bomber to Zurich, where the entire crew was interned." Intrigued, and wanting to know more, Mears wrote to the Swiss government requesting information. He recalls:

> I found out that my grandfather had been incarcerated in a prison camp for attempting to escape back to Allied lines in France. The camp, Wauwilermoos, had notoriously poor conditions: the prisoners slept on lice-infested straw, were malnourished and had virtually no hygiene facilities or access to medical care. The camp was surrounded by barbed-wire and patrolled by armed guards with dogs. After the war, Switzerland even prosecuted the pro-Nazi commander of the camp. Learning of my grandfather's captivity in Wauwilermoos was the

114 • PRISONER OF THE SWISS

genesis of my desire to recognize him with the Prisoner of War Medal. Later, after I interacted with many internees who shared similar experiences, I realized that it would be a more meaningful achievement to bestow this recognition on those airmen who were still alive to receive it.

Thus began a 15-year journey for the younger Mears. Early in his recognition efforts, Mears found that the POW Medal had already been presented to Dan Culler in 1996 with the assistance of USAF Chief of Staff Gen. Ronald Fogleman. Culler provided Mears his paperwork and several affidavits about the camp, but the Army and the Air Force refused to recognize the medal as a precedent. The military eventually disavowed the medal and claimed that it was "erroneously awarded." The military also refused to recognize other precedents, such as previous awards to 291 World War II airmen held in the USSR (which was neutral in the Pacific theater), and several associated legal reviews that agreed with Mears's interpretation of the law. Mears documented over 400 cases where awards officials had endorsed internees, detainees, and hostages for the POW Medal, but every application he made was treated differently.

The issue was the military's interpretation of the POW Medal statute, which was created in 1985 as part of the FY1986 National Defense Authorization Act. The original statute strictly required captivity by a declared belligerent in formal armed conflict with the United States. This quickly led to controversy, because the law excluded all internees, detainees, and hostages held outside of formal conflict. Senator Alan Cranston, chairman of the Committee on Veterans' Affairs, proposed an amendment to cover "those individuals who were held captive in neutral or allied countries," as well as "the crewmembers of the U.S.S. *Pueblo* and the military personnel who were held captive in Iran during the seizure of the United States Embassy in Tehran." Cranston's amendment was incorporated into the FY1990 National Defense Authorization Act, allowing some captives held outside of armed conflict to receive the medal. Specifically, the amendment authorized captives held "by foreign armed forces that are hostile to the United States, under circumstances which the Secretary concerned finds to have been comparable to those under which persons have generally been held captive by enemy armed forces during periods of armed conflict." In the conference report accompanying the act, the Committee on Armed Services mentioned that the amendment was "intended to cover the individuals taken prisoner as a result of the U.S.S. *Pueblo* seizure, as well as any similar occurrence that the Service Secretary concerned deems comparable to the circumstances under which persons have generally been held captive by enemy armed forces during a war or conflict."

In Mears's view, the problem was the military's interpretation of this law:

> Internees were considered ineligible for this medal because they were held by a neutral country, and the existing law required captivity by a belligerent in a declared conflict, or alternately captivity by "foreign armed forces hostile to the United States." The Wauwilermoos airmen subjectively met neither qualification, although their treatment was comparable to captivity during declared conflicts. I felt strongly that this decoration was intended to recognize the personal sacrifices of service members in captivity, not merely the diplomatic relationship with their captors.

Mears refused to give up. He first applied through the Army for six years. The Office of the Judge Advocate General of the Army concluded that they had "no legal objection to the award of the Prisoner of War Medal to 1LT Mears," and believed that his conditions of captivity in Switzerland met the legal requirement of being "comparable to those generally experienced by persons held prisoner by enemy armed forces during periods of armed conflict." However, the Office of the Assistant Secretary of the Army rejected the award on the basis that "the mistreatment at the Wauwilermoos camp did not create a condition in which Switzerland lost its neutrality and became an opposing or foreign armed force hostile to the United States." Further, the Assistant Secretary claimed that "to award the POW medal to those service members held by neutral countries would alter the nature of the sacrifice that the medal represents," implying that it would denigrate the sacrifices of other, more deserving, POWs. The ruling was based on a biased and unscholarly historical advisory that claimed "giving the medal to those who were interned in 'The Swiss Theater of Inactivity,' as it was called by the detainees, lessens the sacrifice of those men who underwent

116 • PRISONER OF THE SWISS

intense suffering at the hands of the Japanese, and those who endured life in a German camp."

Mears next took his case to the Air Force Board for Correction of Military Records (BCMR), where it was similarly rejected on the dubious basis that the pertinent Geneva Convention prohibited the award to internees because the treaty defined POWs as captives of belligerents during declared international armed conflicts. Mears scrutinized the legal opinion cited by the BCMR, and realized that it was based on the outdated POW Medal statute that strictly required captivity by a declared belligerent during armed conflict. He wrote to the former Air Force Assistant General Counsel who authored the legal opinion, and the attorney agreed that internees should be eligible for the award. The former General Counsel authored a written retraction affirming that his legal opinion was "outdated by enactment of Public Law 101-189, November 29, 1989," and agreed that "there is ample legal authority and precedent for the award of the POW medal to US military personnel held as internees by Switzerland during World War II." The BCMR repeatedly refused to reconsider Mears's case even with the written support of the former General Counsel and two congressmen who were involved in authoring the POW Medal statute. BCMR officials claimed that discovery of the incorrect legal basis for the reject was "not adequate grounds for reopening a case."

Mears next applied to the BCMR on behalf of over a dozen other airmen held in Wauwilermoos, but few of these cases ever received a hearing. He later discovered that the BCMR had terminated most of the cases he submitted, apparently in violation of their own procedures. According to Mears:

> ... this was not surprising to me at all, because I had already observed that BCMR officials were perfectly willing to overlook the law and regulations, and they apparently had little to no oversight. In hindsight, I think they were irritated by the fact that I raised legitimate questions about their legal opinions, and they certainly were not used to that level of scrutiny. From that point on their responses to my research were thoroughly unprofessional, and this convinced me that the BCMR was not a level playing field; it was a forum where officials only sporadically maintained the illusion of due process.

On his many petitions to the Army and Air Force, Mears said the following:

> ... the 'experts' repeatedly denied all of my submissions, but were never able to explain the rejections in a manner that seemed honest to the law governing the medal or the history of how the airmen were treated. I consistently received form-letter rejections that parroted incorrect history and law, which led me to question the integrity of the awards process. I eventually concluded that the bureaucracy was incapable of unraveling the history of the internment in Switzerland, the legislative history of the controlling statute, or the policy governing the award. It was obvious that much of the history was distorted, the policy proponents had no continuity files, and most lower-level government attorneys seemed completely unaware that the controlling law even existed.

In early 2011 Mears found records proving that the Department of Defense (DoD) policy on the medal was incorrectly based on a statute that was repealed in 1989, meaning that this outdated policy could not be cited as grounds to deny the medal.

The records proved that "personnel policy officials at the Office of the Secretary of Defense had failed to implement any policy for the POW Medal amendment in the Fiscal Year 1990 Defense Bill. Further, they had discovered the mistake in 1991, but did little to remedy it, and as a result the incorrect policy was perpetuated for decades among all of the services." In particular, service and DoD policy incorrectly claimed that "hostages of terrorists and persons detained by governments with which the United States is not engaged actively in armed conflict are not eligible for the POW Medal," which directly contradicted the controlling law. Mears's findings were definitive, but they still failed to sway military personnel policy officials.

After over a decade of petitions, Mears realized that he had little chance of success with the bureaucracy, and so he channeled his efforts into publishing his research and amending the law controlling the medal. "I found traction with the House Committee on Armed Services," he wrote, "as well as with several retired Air Force officials." In 2010, the Committee on Armed Services responded to Mears's research and directed the Office of the Secretary of Defense (OSD) to review the policy behind the award. In 2011, OSD informed the Committee that internees did not qualify for the award because "Switzerland was a neutral country and Switzerland's armed forces were not hostile to the United States." Mears critiqued this claim as a "Catch-22," noting that the statute did not require hostility by the entire host country, but merely the persons most directly holding and mistreating U.S. captives. Further, the hostility provision was impossible to satisfy, because it was not precisely defined in the law or policy.

As a result, "an internee who appealed for the POW Medal based on hostile captivity—such as mistreatment in Wauwilermoos—was told he did not qualify because he was not held by a hostile force, and he could never receive the medal because he could never be held by a hostile force no matter how hostile his treatment." Mears noted that the problem was the DoD's slippery interpretation of neutrality, under which "neutral captivity negated all hostility unless the United States declared war against the neutral state." Yet a declaration of war was not a prerequisite for the medal, since "the 1989 amendment overturned the requirement for captivity by a declared enemy, meaning that a hostile force was a nonbelligerent because it could not be interpreted as an 'enemy' or an 'opposing foreign force' as defined by the original statute."

When Mears sent his research to Congress he also contacted the former General Counsel of the Air Force, who endorsed several hundred internees of Siberia for the award in 1992. The General Counsel agreed with Mears's interpretation of the law, and helped him to circulate his research to current and former Air Force leadership. This ultimately led to what Mears called "an unlikely amendment in the Fiscal Year 2013 Defense Bill," which was endorsed by U.S. Air Force Chief of Staff Mark A. Welsh III, Acting Secretary of the Air Force Eric K. Fanning, as well as several prominent veterans' organizations. In authoring the amendment, the Committee on Armed Services reported that "some internees have been awarded the medal, while the vast majority have not. In the conferees' view, this is the result of inconsistent interpretations of provisions of the current law that would be removed by this provision."

On January 3, 2013, President Barack Obama signed the Fiscal Year 2013 Nation Defense Authorization Act. Section 584 of the act modified Title 10, Section 1128, to allow award of the POW Medal "to any person who, while serving in any capacity with the armed forces, was held captive under circumstances not covered by the [1985 statute], but which the Secretary concerned finds were comparable to those circumstances under which persons have generally been held captive by enemy armed forces during periods of armed conflict." The language was similar to that contained in the previous amendment in 1989, except that the Committee removed the ambiguous requirement for captivity by "foreign armed forces hostile to the United States."

The culmination of Mears's efforts came on April 30, 2014, when Air Force Chief of Staff Gen. Mark A. Welsh presented the Prisoner of War Medal to 143 airmen interned during World War II in the Wauwilermoos, Switzerland, prison camp during a Pentagon ceremony. Attending the ceremony and receiving the POW medals in person were eight surviving airmen; a ninth had passed away shortly before the ceremony and the award was accepted by family members.

General Mark A. Welsh III honored the men, who knew that in 1943 and early 1944, the chances of surviving a 25-mission tour of duty over Europe were about one in four. "It's the kind of courage we read about in books, that people make movies about and that these humble, grateful survivors praise on their fallen comrades, but rarely seem to recognize in themselves," Welsh said. "But make no mistake about it—these men have that kind of courage … They served each other and our country proudly. They saved a world and they inspired a nation."

In the end, "This became a matter of principle for me," wrote Mears. "The medal itself has little intrinsic value, but I persisted because it was symbolic of reversing the stigma associated with internment, in particular the insulting perception that these men were cowards and unworthy of decorations of any kind." In his view, "that the internees deserved this recognition was self-evident to anyone who knew the facts. They just needed someone to advocate for them, and I was privileged to fill that role." Although clearly disillusioned by the intransigence of military awards officials, Mears believed that the experience was ultimately redeeming. He reflected that "no matter the outcome, this journey enabled me to perform some fascinating research and help many to learn about the experiences of their loved ones." He also believed "the ceremony demonstrated that the Air Force leadership strongly supported these airmen and appreciated their sacrifices. I owe them and many of their predecessors a debt for making this day happen."

Selected Bibliography and Sources

Culler, Dan. *Black Hole of Wauwilermoos*. Green Valley, AZ: Circle of Thorns Press. 1995.

Culler, Dan. *Circle of Thorns: Birth and the Learning Years*. Green Valley, AZ: Circle of Thorns Press. 1992.

Culler, Dan. Interviews over a 14-year period, 2000–14.

Egger, Dani. Swiss historian, for selected photos and information.

King, Norris. Swiss internee, for selected photos and information.

Mears, Major Dwight. Interviews and correspondence, 2014.

Morris, Rob. *Untold Valor: Forgotten Stories of American Bomber Crewmen over Europe in World War II*. Dulles, VA: Potomac Books, 2006.

Silkett, Wayne A. "Armed but neutral was Switzerland's war policy—despite occasional air combat or errant bombs." *Armament Magazine*. 1993. pp. 16, 63–66.

Thomas, Roy. Son of Swiss Internee, for selected photos and information.

Wyss, Daniel. Swiss film producer, for selected photos and information.